THE LOVE-RESPONSE HELPER

WAYNE LINDSEY

The Love-Response Helper
From Darkness to Light

First published in 2018 by
Panoma Press Ltd
48 St Vincent Drive, St Albans, Herts, AL1 5SJ UK
info@panomapress.com
www.panomapress.com

Printed and bound by TJ International Ltd, Padstow, Cornwall

Cover design by Neil Coe
Artwork by Karen Gladwell

ISBN 978-1-784521-43-1

A CIP catalogue record for this book is available from the British Library.

In loving memory

Warren Anthony Salisbury
August 1988 – September 2017

You may be gone but never forgotten. I know you are smiling down on us, saying everything is okay.
R.I.P. My Homie

Contents

Author personal mottos

All human beings deserve some form of happiness in their lives, even if it is only for a short spell of their lifetime. **Wayne Lindsey**

Be clear about the goals that can bring you happiness, stay committed and focus on them. **Wayne Lindsey**

Be driven, determined and dedicated to finding success and a healthy wellbeing. **Wayne Lindsey**

Be ambitious, but do not belittle others once you have achieved success. **Wayne Lindsey**

Remove all doubts from your mind and strive to reach your goal. Always tell yourself that you are TBE, "The Best Ever." **Floyd Mayweather Jr**

Never compare yourself to others; you may become bitter and vain. **Max Ehrmann**

Acknowledgments

I have been particularly grateful in the preparation of this book for the interest shown by Nick Cooke, who has over 25 years' experience as a clinical practitioner and over 12 years' experience as a trainer, and thank him for his guidance, insightful feedback, support and ideas.

I give my continuous thanks to Melanie Tinker, a qualified librarian, who also runs a successful virtual administration business, who helped by typing and proofreading.

I am immensely grateful to John, Paula and Thomas for sharing and allowing their stories to be detailed in this book.

With the assistance of these lovely people, this book will continue to bring more happiness than hurt.

To you all, my grateful thanks.

WL

Preface

The purpose of this book is to help people who experience unpleasant abuse such as physical, verbal, sexual and other abuse. If this book doesn't provide such help, then this book did not serve its purpose.

This love-response book provides tools you need to release your fears, overcome anger, embrace self-acceptance, transform anger into compassion, connect and strengthen your natural abilities to heal.

This book's primary aim is to develop a person's self-awareness and self-esteem by asking self-reflective questions, such as:

- Are you afraid? Of what?
- Are you hurt by someone?
- Are you feeling worthless?
- Are you feeling resentment?
- Are you feeling insignificant?
- Do you feel you will never experience true love?

This love-response book will teach you:

- How to heal and open your heart.
- How to develop coping skills that will enable you to handle challenging times in your life.
- How to turn abuse hurt into happiness.
- How to turn off physical effects of fear, low self-esteem, and emotional hurt from the past and turn on positive, healthy wellbeing.
- How to feel motivated and inspired.
- How to increase your cognitive function.
- How to feel physically vibrant and emotionally balanced.
- How to heal the abused minds, moods and memories.
- How to feel in control of your life and body.
- To have a clear clarity of mind and spirit.

After reading this book if you feel joy, happiness, peace and love, then this book has fulfilled its purpose. This book is about the suffering and hope in which our lives are filled. It is about the true authenticity of happiness and love we crave.

Introduction

All human beings have an intense desire to be loved and nurtured. The need to be loved, as Bowlby's and others' experiments have shown, could be considered one of our basic and fundamental needs.

Many people suffer abuse silently and secretly for years. Sometimes they feel too ashamed or guilty to reveal their problems to anyone and struggle to overcome their past abuse and hurt.

The love-response and self-help approach provides the framework, tools and techniques for a lifeline recovery to eradicate our body of emotional effects of stresses, overcoming hurtful past life events, and heals the abused both internally and externally for a better future.

Part One

The Love-Response Helper

Where I stand

My philosophical beliefs for us to have true happiness in our daily lives and self-help healing are strongly influenced by the love-response approach.

Because techniques and procedures of the love-response are of an eclectic approach, the love-response gives freedom to integrate various psychotherapeutic models of therapy to help people who are stressed, lonely, abused, have low self-worth and so on.

Some therapeutic theoretical models which can be used with love-response are:

Bowlby's: Attachment theories

ACT: Acceptance commitment therapy

CBT: Cognitive behavior therapy

PCT: Person-centered therapy

MBCT: Mindfulness-based cognitive therapy

MBSR: Mindfulness-based stress reduction

An opinion of mine is that the low self-worth person can accept and commit to the healing of emotional and behavioral difficulties. However, their social, toxic environment and cultural hurdles might hinder them. What could be crucial in hindering the love-response is for the person to cope with the internal and external forces that could stifle their behavior. A person who suffers low self-esteem, loneliness and fear will become discouraged and need love encouragement for life-changing positive growth to build significant future relationships.

Love-response can help the abused people who suffer depression, low self-esteem, etc. to revitalize significant changes in their lives; they can make decisions about how they would like to change and re-shape their life. For me, practicing love-response can develop our awareness of:

a. Caring: Who really cares for me? How is care shown to me?

b. Emotions: What to do about my emotions when I am feeling frustrated and when I am in public places? Do I try to hide them or some of them? Am I moody?

c. Intimacy: What does intimacy mean to me? What kind of intimacy do I find 1) most rewarding, 2) most threatening?

The love-response shows us how to transform our lives by transforming hatred into love, hurt into joy, and fear into self-belief.

Remember, "unless you love someone, nothing else makes sense." E.E. Cummings.

What is love-response?

The love-response is the result of Dr. Eva M. Selhub's year of research and clinical practice on how to reverse the destructive physical effects of fear and stress and banish emotional wounds from the past through a simple to use plan of awareness, breathing, visualization, and verbal command exercises. The love-response reprograms your brain and changes your biochemistry from negative to positive, putting you on a path to long-term wellness and happiness.

The love-response is structured and the essential building blocks of mental health:

- Social-love: deep, intimate relationships including family, friends, and pets.
- Self-love: how to nurture yourself, often the hardest step.
- Spiritual-love: contributing to the world beyond your own needs.

Love-response helps you to recognize that reading about health, balance and resilience is not enough.

When we put the theory into practice, we become competent to heal ourselves.

Love-response is an eight-week program designed to help you to cope with stress, develop resilience and learn to counteract the unhealthy effects of fear and stress with techniques that can lead to multiple benefits including better health, improved problem-solving, clearer thinking and emotional balance.

The love-response eight-week program covers:

- Session 1: choosing to use stress, not lose it
- Session 2: the love pyramid (self, social, and spiritual love)
- Session 3: the heart connection
- Session 4: shifting from fear to trust
- Session 5: from anger to compassion
- Session 6: from judgment to acceptance
- Session 7: from half to whole
- Session 8: from 'I' to 'we'

What the love-response does

The love-response provides all the tools you need to transform:

- Your strength, a natural ability to heal.
- Anger into compassion.
- Loss, separation or divorce when you are finding it difficult to cope.

- Our connection through empathy.
- A deeper level of learning, order, action and release.
- Release pent-up thoughts and emotions.
- Allows you to heal relationships.
- Brings out natural beauty and wisdom.
- It reveals, tracks patterns and cycles.
- Helps clarify thoughts, feelings, and behaviors.
- Helps you identify your values.
- Helps you find more meaning in life.
- Eases decision making.
- Improves families and friendship unity.
- Soothes troubled memories.
- Helps you write your own journal.
- Stimulates significant changes.
- Helps you feel unstuck from an inconsolable sadness.
- Provides clear insights.
- It is motivational.
- Offers positive perspectives.
- Helps you find peace in your life.
- Sharpens the mind.
- Helps you plan a constructive course of action to solve a problem.
- Promotes satisfying relationships with peers.

- Helps you to stop believing that you are useless.
- Makes you behave more assertively.
- Gives you inner harmony.
- Holds thoughts still so they can be changed and integrated.

The key to love-response

Love can begin in many ways with smiles, whispers or a glance. It continues with hugs, kisses, sometimes frowns and arguments. It ends with sadness, frustration, rage and tears, or maybe joy and laughter. It can last for a day, month or endure for years and beyond death.

Love-response is something we look for, or it finds us. It can be our salvation or our ruin.

Humans yearn for love, are impelled to it. But we are still puzzled by the understanding of love. What makes love stop? Why do we pursue love? What makes it persist? What does it mean to love, to have a loving relationship? Does love make any sense at all? These are questions we normally ask.

Today we have cracked the code of love. We now know what a good love relationship looks and feels like. Even better, we can shape it; we have a map that can guide us in creating, healing and sustaining love.

John Bowlby, a British psychiatrist who is the father of attachment theory, a developmental perspective on personality that puts our emotions and our interactions with loved ones front center in terms of who we are and how we behave.

Bowlby was passionate about the importance of love attachments between children and parents and other significant adults. He pioneered on giving form to a theory of what he called "attachment" (the story goes that when asked by his wife why didn't he give it its rightful name, a theory of love, he replied, "I would be laughed out of science").

Bowlby was aided significantly in his work by psychologist Mary Ainsworth, a Canadian researcher who helped give shape to his ideas and test them. Together they identified four elements of attachment:

- We seek out, monitor and try to maintain emotional and physical connection with our loved ones. Throughout life, we rely on them to be emotionally accessible, responsive and engaged with us.
- We reach out for our loved ones particularly when we are uncertain, threatened, anxious or upset. Contact with them gives us a sense of having a safe haven, where we will find comfort and emotional support; this sense of safety teaches us how to regulate our own emotions and how to connect with and trust others.
- We miss our loved ones and become extremely upset when they are physically or emotionally remote; this perception anxiety can become intense and incapacitating. Isolation is inherently traumatizing for human beings.

- We depend on our loved ones to support us emotionally and be a secure base as we venture into the world and learn and explore. The more we sense that we are effectively connected, the more autonomous and separate we can be.

The basic concept of those elements is that forming a deep mutual bond with another is the first imperative of the human species and considered to be the norm and universal, occurring in relationships across culture. Bowlby's theory was missing empirical evidence; however, Mary Ainsworth came to his rescue – she devised a simple and genius experiment that is regarded as one of the most important and influential in all of psychology.

When we do not love, we feel unworthy of love, but we should not take that the wrong way. Every person is worthy of love. There are no conditions on that. You are worthy of love, abundant love, infinite love, no matter what you do or don't do.

Here, when we speak of unworthiness, we are talking not of an objective fact but of a subjective feeling. Do we feel worthy of love? Subjectively it is difficult for a person who is not meeting their own love standards to feel love-worthy. Instead, we tend to feel that people are making a mistake in trying to love us. The result is we can't actually receive the love we are given.

So you see, there is really no solution to the sorrow of feeling unloved until we ourselves are willing to love, be cared for and understood; otherwise we close our doors to receiving the very love we feel resentful about not getting, and we live in sorrow. The only way for those doors to be opened is to love enough and to do unto others as we would have done unto us.

The continuity of love and intimacy depends on honesty, not on mood. In this shifting world where moods and circumstances change all of the time, the only possible answer is honesty. Honesty is the only base that you stand on. If you try to base a relationship on the constancy of mood, believing that it should always be hearts and flowers, that it should always be wonderful, you will soon find you have taken a wrong turn. You have moved from what was real to what is now fake.

What was once fantastic and beautiful will become sickening and disappointing in the heart as soon as it is no longer true. But truthfulness can make us beautiful.

Truthfulness is a great rectifier of life; it cleans out the untrue from the true, the beautiful from the ugly. It makes those crucial distinctions upon which heart satisfaction depends.

Honesty is an upward spiral toward a truly beautiful life. The reason most people doubt that is because so often a meeting will start out honest but lose the trail somewhere in the middle. Someone got defensive. Someone got offensive. And so you walk away from what was supposed to be a truthful meeting shaking your head because it became a mess in the middle, and upset you. The truthful meeting became deeply untruthful.

No truthful person would ever say or believe that you are all bad and wrong. Honesty would also recognize the beauty in you and bring it out. The very process of engaging in a truthful exchange is always liberating, always refining, always improving, ever spiraling upward by the very fact of true discernment between the real and the unreal. That's what it does.

Honesty brings relief to the heart. If you want a secure and true relationship, the only way is truthfulness and honesty. It relieves you when someone tells you a truthful word, and it will relieve you to be able to tell them the truth too. That means, as you go through your day, be there honestly and authentically, tell the truth about each moment as it happens. So be honest, be consistent in that, and the truth will set you free.

Love-response connections

Humans are social beings. Some of us like a little solitude now and again, but even introverts need to feel connected, cared for and understood. Our DNA compels us to seek relationships that satisfy those needs.

Our biological need for connection may stem from the survival instinct. But love and connection provide much deeper benefits than a simple response to the instinct to survive. Positive love relationships contribute to better physical and mental health, longevity and happiness. Although the love relationship we have with our families, partners and close circle of friends is essential to our wellbeing and life fulfillment, feeling connected with our community members or at work also contributes to our happiness.

You may not class your social connections as love, but when nurtured, they can stimulate a physical and emotional response that mirrors the benefits of close personal relationships. The fact is social connections are as important to our survival as food and shelter. In fact, positive love relationships are one of the strongest predictions of life satisfaction. Even people with large sums of money, health, and good careers confess that they are not happy unless they have strong, loving relationships.

It's not just emotional wellness that love connections confer; it helps with social isolation and loneliness which are deadly, just like smoking, alcohol and other negative factors that can harm our health.

But if loneliness and social isolation hurts, love and companionship heals, boosting both our health and our happiness.

Love is a constant process of tuning in, connecting, missing and misreading cues, disconnecting, receiving and finding deeper connections. It is a dance of meeting and parting and finding each other day by day.

In terms of mental health, close love connection is the strongest prediction of happiness.

Love is the source of ethics

Love blows like a mighty wind in our heart and soul. It offers us a dynamic life full of energy and inspiration, a life powered by divine will, response and understanding.

Whenever you see real life or real beauty, you see the effects of the love-response. Like the rustling of leaves or the drifting of clouds, the most beautiful creation of humanity, the most inspired social movements, the sweetest smiles, the most loving gestures are all manifestations of the love-response.

Love-response provides us with the compassion, the beauty, the wisdom, the understanding, the positive energy, and the aspiration we need for this moment.

Love is the source of ethics, is it not? If people want loving relationships of any kind at any level to work, then the answer is ethics. And guess what? The main source of true ethics is love. Love is the only element that sufficiently transcends self-interest to allow for a truly ethical orientation, a truly self-sacrificing orientation.

So now we understand ethics counts and love is its cause. That is the magic formula, the key to success for humanity and there is no other. In other words, when it comes to love, and the high ethics that love allows for, there is no replacement in the basement. That is the truth.

Can't you just feel how ethical failures are the number one cause of failed relationships, failed loves? It happens even in the marital bed when one person puts their own pleasure ahead of their lover's pleasure. It happens when someone deceives, does not keep agreement or promises, and withholds love, energy, and attention.

Whenever someone ignores what would be right for their friends, companions, lovers, it will dishearten all who hear of it. And it will cause their associates to lose faith in them, and lose affinity for them. That's what causes the breakdown of friendships, families and business partnerships. It causes breakdown on every level you can name. And again, this is because unethical behaviors and values are hated by humankind.

The things we think and do affect us, that's inevitable. We keep telling ourselves "I will live a better life" and "I will love and be a good person," which is a great inspiration, but the problem is they will not live better that way, because the unloving things they are doing now are keeping them from ever changing their lifestyle. Their present lifestyle is too shy on love and too strong on selfishness, and that depresses our heart.

Human desires are powerful forces. You can declare "I want this to make me happy," but you cannot force it to be so. Likewise, you can declare "I don't want this to make me happy," but you can't stop it from making you happy if it does. And that is why we can't get happy living the evil life, and we can't get happy refusing to live the good life.

It is easy to get happy, is it not? There are some things you could do anytime, that would lift you up and make you genuinely happy. As a person who knows yourself well, you know what those things are. So why not do those things, perhaps even regularly?

Everyone wants to be happy, don't they? A happy life is beautiful, amazing and fulfilling. We only have to follow our hearts and our conscience, we open up to life and let happiness flood in.

You can see it in the lives of some people you know. When a person does wrong, unless they decide to fix it, they will quickly distance themselves from everyone they love. They no longer want to be happy, because it just doesn't seem fitting. And if you reach out to them in such a compressed state, you will have a hard time getting through.

On the other hand, when a person is living rightfully and beautifully, they become bright and happy. They are outgoing. They want to talk. They want to relate closely to people. They become permeable to love and become robust by receiving love and exchanging love in helpful, meaningful, uplifting ways.

We owe it to ourselves to live happy, eternally.

How love-response regulates your body

Love-response can help our emotions decide whether or how neurons fire and wire to produce structural change in the brain.

Activated by our perceptions, emotions are powerful energies that direct the dynamic process in the body. Together, emotions and interpretive thought:

- Stimulate the basic cells of the brain, neurons, to fire in particular patterns.
- Produce physiological sensations felt throughout the physical body.
- Sculpt the synaptic connections of your brain.
- Shape the actions you take or whether you take actions at all.
- Release hormones into the bloodstream that affect the balance of the body's systems.

Emotions of empathy, joy or gratitude are examples of core emotional states of love-response. Whereas emotions of hurt, disappointment and shame are examples of core emotional states of fear. For example, if you decide to focus on faults or self-blame this will likely produce painful feelings inside that are rooted in fear, whereas a focus on working well to achieve a happier lifestyle will likely energize inner feelings rooted in love, which are pleasant.

Love-response helps us make significant changes in our lives by changing from half to a whole you. It helps you practice healthy functioning.

Healthy functioning in Carl Rogers' terms is an effective self-concept for healthy functioning, just as ego strength is, in psychodynamic terms, essential for a sound psyche. A completely effective self-concept will not be at odds with the actualizing tendency of the organismic self; the two will be congruent. An effective self-concept allows us to perceive experience realistically; it will ensure that a person behaves rationally and responsibly. People who are moving toward self-actualization accept responsibility for their own actions and growth.

Think for a moment of how often we say things like "whenever it rains heavy it makes me sad." A responsible, rational person (in Rogers' sense) would be trying to think more along the lines of "I allow the heavy downpour of the rain to make me feel sad." The fact is rationally, the "heavy downpour" can't force us to be sad. We need to acknowledge that we allow ourselves to get upset and accept personal responsibility for this.

Unhealthy functioning can block a person's self-actualizing tendency and now that, in turn, perpetuates unhealthy functioning.

To be self-actualizing seems so gratifying, at such a deep level, that we may wonder why more people are not self-actualizing more often. Our perception, or the selective ways in which we extract and interpret information from our environment, can offer some explanation for this.

The love-response helps us to change anger into compassion. Learning to explore feelings is like learning a new language. However, the more we practice this new language and the more we converse with new speakers, the easier the language becomes. The same is true in developing empathy. Empathy means:

- Tapping into a person's intuition.
- The ability to step into the inner world of another person and to step out again while remaining ourselves.
- Trying to understand the thoughts, feelings, behaviors and personal meanings from a person's frame of reference.
- A fundamental principle in person-centered counselling.
- Working within the conditional framework of another person.
- Communicating non-verbally through facial expressions.
- Not assuming what another person means.

Empathy has different development stages. Martin Hoffman (1982) proposed that the development of empathy is linked to cognitive development and that it occurs in four stages.

1. Global empathy: during the first year of life, an infant shows empathy through its behaviors,

such as crying when it hears another baby crying. This could be that the infant is still egocentric and therefore unable to distinguish between itself and others. Hoffman says this empathetic response is due to either inborn tendencies toward empathy or early classical conditioning.

2. Egocentric empathy: toddlers respond to the feelings of others, so they will try to comfort a crying child, or show fear when another child is frightened.
3. Empathy for anothers' feelings: children start to show they can identify other's feelings and respond in a certain way, i.e., they may try to mend a broken toy or doll, or wipe up spilt juice.
4. Empathy for another's general plight: children begin to recognize the implications of someone else's situation; for example, victims of storms and earthquakes.

The love-response eight-session program allows a person to:

- Become motivated.
- Reflect on situations.
- Evaluate vital information.
- Expand their awareness.
- Increase their understanding of human behavior.
- Stimulate critical thinking.

- Improve self-esteem.
- Relieve emotional pressure.

The love-response helps us to know our core values which are part of living an authentic life. When we live from our core values, we are able to find more meaning in our lives. Here are a few core values which play significant roles in our lives:

- Achievement.
- Adventurousness.
- Ambition.
- Assertiveness.
- Belonging.
- Bravery.
- Cheerfulness.
- Decisiveness.
- Diversity.
- Enjoyment.
- Faith.
- Focus.
- Fun.
- Happiness.
- Honesty.
- Success.
- Understanding.
- Unity.

The feelings of trust and connection that this hormone stimulates automatically reverse into the bloodstream. Our brain is all about relationships; thus, our deepest strivings are for love and meaningful connection to life with and around you. This explains why love for yourself and others enhances your sense of security — and why some of our greatest fears have to do with loss of love and disconnect. As an adult, early protective neural patterns no longer serve us.

We are wired to form certain protective patterns in the first years of life. Once set, these habituated protective response patterns operate, for the most part, without conscious awareness.

Whenever we experience reoccurring problems, emotional sufferings in our lives or addictive compulsions it is likely connected to these early neural patterns that essentially prevent our conscious mind (logic) and subconscious mind (emotions) from working together.

The body's survival reaction, which is more commonly known as the flee response, hijacks our capacity to freely choose our thoughts and actions. When this occurs, it is as if our power to make choices gets switched off. Disconnected from the power of choice, you naturally may feel a sense of powerlessness, helplessness or loss of control and then blame others or isolate to get a quic-fix. So often, it appears the very things we most need to heal are what we most fear and avoid, and simultaneously, the very things we most need to let go of and consciously release are the things we crave.

The story of Paula

In this love-response chapter, the following are three live case stories of Paula, John and Thomas who have been through neglect, abuse and detachment and have now found self-love, social love, and spiritual love through eight weeks of successful therapeutic sessions. Let's take a look at these case stories.

Paula

I have never really had much luck when it comes to family, especially in my childhood.

I was born to a drug-addicted mother, who would always be off her face on whatever she could get her hands on, be that drugs or alcohol. She was out of control, violent, constantly on the hunt for the next thing she was going to steal or person she was going to rob, not to provide for her children, but to pay for her drugs.

I remember quite a lot from my early years when I was still with my mom. I think the earliest memory I have is of when my mom went into labor with my little sister; I remember as the ambulance crew came in I felt scared and kept wondering where they were taking my mom. I absolutely adored my little sister though from the second I laid eyes on her.

I tried to protect her. Her dad was just as bad, if not worse when in a temper than my mom. When they argued they would fight and things would start to break/get smashed/thrown, so I used to get my sister and put her in her walker, and we would go out of the house and away from the drama.

I used to enjoy these trips, which is sad when I think about it, but we used to walk down to the convenience store, and the store owner would always be so sweet. I guess she took pity on us, always giving us lots of food to take back (if I remember correctly, she used to walk back with us). The whole area knew what our mom was like and I expect they would have all at one point or another seen my mom or one of her boyfriends leaving in handcuffs or seen social services banging on the door when mom wouldn't send me to school for ages or someone had reported her to them. I'm not surprised we all got taken away. I also have three older sisters that she wasn't able to keep, and most of the four and a half years I was with her she would put me into temporary respite care, usually on a Friday, and would ask for me back on Monday if she could be bothered.

I remember moving a lot with my mom as well; we had over 15 homes, and when I was taken away for good, the home I settled in for the longest was my 18th foster home (not including respite houses). This is a lot of disruption for a young child and led to me having quite bad behavior problems, especially through school.

The only one place that I ever felt like part of a normal family was when I went to live with a family just before my fifth birthday. I still saw my mom when she could be bothered to turn up. They got the very worst of my bad behavior and their biological children obviously weren't happy with that; they used to try, or should I say succeed, at blaming me for things they had done or did things to get me into trouble. They used to say things that would hurt and upset me to try to make me act up.

The one thing I won't ever forget is my foster sister used to sneak into my room at night when I was asleep and blow onto my face. This made me scared to death that there was a ghost in the room and the only reason I knew she was doing this is that one night I saw her running out of my door after it had happened. This may only seem like a small thing to anyone else but to me it had a huge impact, she must have done it a few times when I was around six or seven years old, but once it had stopped I started waking up in the middle of the night and not being able to move or speak and feeling really, really scared, this would happen a lot in my teenage years also.

I wasn't always like this though; I absolutely loved Christmas, it was like I was really part of the family, and not because of the presents, just everyone was so happy and nice to each other, I felt loved and safe. They used to take us on vacations as well, and a lot of the time they were enjoyable. However, my foster carers were very strict, so I often found myself in trouble or being excluded from activities over the tiniest things, even not finishing the last few mouthfuls on my plate, and I was told I was not allowed to do something that all of us kids were looking forward to. If it was her children, it was different rules, and this made it hard for me ever to accept that they loved me as their own, as they tried to tell other people they did.

Once I hit my teenage years, I really spiraled out of control. It started in school when I was nine; my mom died from a drug overdose one week after I told her to drop dead when she phoned me as it was the first contact I had had since I was five or six, the hurt always stays with me for that. Then throughout school two of my good friends passed away, I didn't take it all too well; I ended up getting permanently excluded from school and being put into out of school education, where they put all the naughty kids. By age 11-12 I was smoking cannabis, absconding from the school unit with other kids and stealing all sorts in stores and just being stupid and getting drunk. In the end spending my time with these sorts of people made me not stick to the boundaries and rules my foster carers had in place, and I used to stay at a friend's most of the week.

Then they had to call the police, and I was taken back, so I ran away for good, aged 12, and went to live with a friend and her alcoholic mom and older brother. It was all okay until my friend and I fell out, and I had nowhere else to go. I was devastated; she was like a sister to me. I stayed there for almost a year, even spent Christmas there and enjoyed having a true friend and being able to do as I wanted. Before I met her, I had the odd few friends but was bullied quite badly for being in foster care, and I was even tormented after my mom died so a lot of people would avoid the bullies, and as they fooled me into thinking they were friends, people avoided me too, as I stupidly hung about with the nasty girls when they pretended to be nice to me, to corner me, to make it easier to be as horrible as they could.

This friend was different though, I could tell she was genuine, and even though we fell out back then, we are still friends and in touch now. We fell out because her brother used me and denied it once he was found out. As you can imagine, being bullied meant boys didn't really take an interest in me, so I wasn't very knowledgeable in that area. He had realized this and used to call me into his room at night when everyone else was asleep. It started with him giving me compliments; the next few nights were the same, and he would even flirt with me in the day. Then each night he would do more; first it was a kiss, then he started giving me alcohol so he could do more, as at age 13, it didn't take much to get me drunk. When I told his sister, he completely denied it, and once he had what he wanted, he went cold on me and acted like he hated me, which was extremely confusing.

After all this, I had nowhere to live, so I spent 18 months moving to a different house every week, or occasionally I would stay a few weeks, but only if the foster carers didn't kick me out for running away and getting drunk a lot of the time. They all got annoyed with me in the end and the police always bringing me back would get too much, so in the end there wasn't one foster home that would take me in. I had to move into children's homes, and I went through every one in the area by the time I was 15. A lot of my teenage years were spent getting drunk or high and usually arrested because the police would pick me up as a missing person and because I had had a drink I wouldn't go home without a fight. This usually ended up with me getting arrested, and I had a lot of convictions because of this; around that time the police knew me due to always being a missing person.

After doing eight sessions of mindfulness, person-centered counseling and love-response technique with Dwayne, I am now a support worker and a volunteer at Turning Point, a drug and alcohol addiction support center.

The story of John

With John's permission, this is his true-life story. It all began when five-year-old John was raised on a diet of criticism, physical abuse, verbal abuse, humiliation and being ignored and judged. Nothing he did was ever good enough for his parents; it put a lot of self-doubt in his childhood life.

He would lie awake most nights terrified that any mistakes he made would be rewarded the next day with a beating. His parents never read him a bedtime story. He wished that his parents would give him individual tasks each day; it would increase his sense of belonging and act as a catalyst to be more self-responsible. As John got older, he continued to live in a constant state of fear and even kept a journal that looked like a field analysis. On one page he would write things that affected him when the abuse happened, and on another page he would write down the things he desired such as love, warmth, good guidance and so on.

At school John found himself drawn to children who were abused by their parents. He was striving to find an ending to the abuse he received because love, warmth and nurturing would be such an important part of his child development.

John's words: "I seek to receive what I did not get from my parents in other adults, which helped for a short spell, other times it was just a repeating pattern."

After eight sessions of person-centered therapy, plus applying the love-response techniques to John, John has:

- Allowed a healing process to start within him. Healing starts with expecting more from oneself as no individual is under obligation to keep lining themselves up to be belittled or humiliated.

- Come to a self-actualization that he is a child of the universe who deserves to be happy.
- Affirmed to himself that physical, verbal and mental abuse was unhealthy for his brain. The human brain is incredibly adaptive, and in response to an abusive environment it will shut down to protect itself as much as it can from the abuse.
- Taken responsibility for seeing himself as a valuable person.
- Taken a leap of faith and followed his passion to work really hard at college and gain a decent job.

John has now made positive progress in his life by going to college and studying to become an effective drug and alcohol counselor. He is also a volunteer for Acorns Counseling Service.

The story of Thomas

My name is Thomas; I'm 36 years old and I was with my partner for 14 years. This is my story!

I moved when I was 15 years old to live with my mother and sister. You know what parents are like; if I wanted money I had to earn it. I had chores left, right and center, grass cutting being one of them which led to my crush on older women. Most weeks I would be out the front cutting the grass, and this sweet-looking lady would walk past my house in little tops and cut-off hot pants. She had the most slender and toned body, perfect in my eyes, that I had seen. She would look and smile but never spoke. It's like we read each other's minds, she knew exactly what time I would be out front. This went on for a few years. I then went to college, had a couple of relationships, although nothing special.

After leaving college, I moved in with my sister and nephew, who just so happened to live on the same street as the older woman that used to flirt with me, and who I now knew as Liz. I was a young, blond, spiky-haired, blue-eyed boy. I was hot looking, and it was my turn to flirt! I had to go past her house to get to the convenience store and on occasions stopped near enough right outside her house when she was outside. The sensual attraction in the air was massive. On her child's birthday, I walked by, and they invited me in. It was a great day. I was just about to go, and she grabbed my hand and pulled me toward her, the next thing I knew we were in a hot embrace, kissing passionately.

Four months on I had moved in, the relationship was great, the kids loved me, and everything was perfect. I started my own bicycle business, mainly either repairing them for people or building my own in the shed. Three years down the line, the children were older, and Liz and I had started to go clubbing. Drink can change people, which I found out. Even though we were a couple, she would drink and dance and have drunken guys dancing around her and never told them to stop even though I was standing there.

Then the arguments started, we would work through and go back to normal. Then she was invited on a bar tour with her niece. I went out with my sister and her partner, and while in the bar my sister happened to be in the bathroom and in walked Liz, her niece, and a few others, all of them bad-mouthing me behind my back. Then my sister speaks up: "Having fun talking about my brother like that?" She then walked out and told me what had been said.

I let this boil as my mother passed away, which hit my sister and me hard. The nights out got worse, Liz continued to flirt with other men on these nights out, but being so much in love with her, I forgave her.

My drinking got worse, and our relationship started going downhill. I could not see a way past it. Then out of nowhere I decided to quit, went to Turning Point and got the help I needed, and that was that. Four years on I was still off the liquor. Liz fell pregnant, and we were both over the moon. She told her family, and they were happy for us. Disaster struck when Liz was brainwashed by some of her friends and had an abortion. My world turned upside down; the drinking started again, I moved back in with my sister, got on detox and started again.

Being back to my happy-go-lucky self, I landed a job and the tables turned. Liz started to think I was cheating on her. All I was doing was working and providing good service to the customers. The accusations got worse. I let it slide for a while, but then enough was enough. I ended the relationship, which upset her; she thought I never would, but I did. She used to stand outside the place where I worked crying, begging me to sort it out with her, but I stayed strong and said no.

I then went on an eight-week program of mindfulness which was integrated with Logotherapy and the love-response along with homework and daily journals. I am now confident and wiser. I am off the liquor. I am currently doing a course in psychology.

I would highly recommend the love-response, Logotherapy and mindfulness program to anyone who has been in similar situations to me.

Part Two

The Love-Response Pyramid

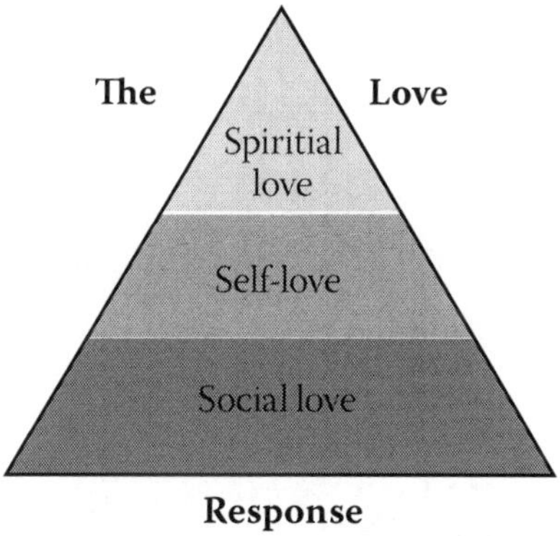

The love-response building blocks of mental health

Self-love

Self-love means learning to perceive yourself without judgment and practicing self-nurture. Taking care of your body with good nutrition and habits, paying attention to physical and emotional needs, and treating yourself the way you would treat someone you love, builds self-confidence and self-esteem to accept yourself just the way you are. This gives you stronger self-control, and your fear response stays dormant more often, keeping physiological responses in check and making you a healthier person.

Some vital prompts for self-love

- What's working in your life?
- What's not working?
- What would you like more of in your life?
- What are you grateful for?

Goals, dreams, visions

- What do you secretly yearn for?
- Describe your ideal day.
- What massive action can you take right now to move you closer to your dreams?
- Write a bio for your future self.

Emotions and energetics

- How do you want to feel?
- When do you feel vibrant, electric and most alive?
- How can you add more love to the world?
- How can you incorporate more fun and more play into your life?
- What could you do to feel more peaceful?

The power to love yourself unconditionally and wholeheartedly lies within you. Your ability to accept, honor, cherish, value and love yourself starts with you.

Here is a tool that makes it easier to focus more time on the inner number one you.

An ultimate self-love journal or diary is an empowerment tool that helps you stay focused and gives you time each day to check in with yourself through writing, meeting your daily or weekly goals in all areas of your life, and an accountability tool to keep you connected to loving yourself and loving your dream life.

In your journal, you will find space to:

- Write responses to self-discovery exercises that get you to focus on how you will honor, cherish and even practice self-forgiveness.
- Release unpleasant thoughts in the name of self-love.
- Acknowledge what you are grateful for at the end of each day.
- Reflect weekly on your self-love journey.
- Map out your days with purpose to help you create a more self-loving and fulfilling life.

BONUS: The pleasure and passion pages can be used to brainstorm self-care ideas, self-esteem, and love.

Self-love – unconditional love

The unconditional loving self doesn't distinguish between right and wrong and has no concept of backward or forward. She's always in the moment, meeting everyone and everything with understanding and compassion. She sees the other as herself, as a deep universal self.

Trying to be unconditional doesn't work because it is life that is unconditional, not the individual. We live in the unconditional, and this allows us the freedom to create conditions. Humanity, as it goes along, has always created collective cultural and societal norms, and as individuals, we impose specific conditions on ourselves and others all of the time.

Sometimes we confuse ourselves and act as though unconditional love is unconditional giving, so in our efforts to be unconditionally loving we give and give right up until the moment resentment, frustration and anger kick in, and we can suppress these painful emotions no more. But true unconditional love is not unconditional giving. It's unconditional acceptance of our imagined imperfect selves, of the things within ourselves and others that we dislike and judge as unacceptable.

When we are in love, an unconditional love where anything goes, love is life, and life is unconditional love, allowing all to be the way it is, we made it and are made of it. We were born in it, we live our lives in it, and we will die in it.

Social love

Social love is the base of the love pyramid because your connection with other people defines what it means to be human. The love between you and others sustains you and gives your life reason and meaning.

And without intimacy between two people, you would not exist. Learning to give love and receive love from others serves as a model for giving and receiving love to and from yourself and spirit. Above all, social love affords your physical affection (embracing, holding, caring, touching), a necessary part of keeping the fear response in check.

Stars in your eyes, butterflies in your stomach, weak at the knees; sharing social love is a feeling like no other. But did you know experiencing social love has tangible health benefits for both your body and mind?

Baran Kilical, a cardiologist at Anne Arundel Medical Center, stated, "We are social creatures, and we do our best when we have strong social support systems."

Here are a few of the scientifically backed benefits of experiencing social love.

- **A healthy heart**

  It's fitting that the symbol for love is a heart; people who share social love experience half the risk from heart disease than that of people who isolate themselves.

  According to Dr. Kilical "our sympathetic nervous system, or our stress fight or flight response likely plays a role as well." Being loved tends to decrease our stress response, which in turn can lower blood pressure. The same holds true for heart rate.

- **Healthy lungs**

  It's not just your heart that benefits from being in love or sharing love in groups, with friends or associates. It can help protect against complications and death from pneumonia.

- **Reduce stress**

  Besides the physical health benefits, social love works wonders for your mental health as well, which also strengthens your immune system. According to Dr. Kilical, "love causes changes in many of your hormones including oxytocin, vasopressin, dopamine, serotonin, cortisol, and testosterone." Here's some of what goes on in your brain:

  - The hormones oxytocin and vasopressin interact with your dopamine reward system. This is the same system that causes people to feel good or happy when positive events happen, such as getting a pay rise or enjoying a nice vacation.
  - Vasopressin helps control blood pressure.

Cortisol, the stress hormone, initially rises when you experience love, but quickly drops in a long-term, stable friendship. Low cortisol levels contribute to many health benefits.

Sharing social love is the foremost feeling that rules the world. It takes various forms and serves various purposes. Love is an enormous emotion and the reason for many other emotions that breed from it. What differentiates love from everything else is that it is experienced by all living beings on planet Earth.

In times of hardship and adversity, love prevails and helps a person overcome it with poise and grace. Social love has taken various forms in the life of an individual. A tender touch by a mother, a helping hand by a father, a passionate kiss by a soulmate, an affectionate touch by a brother/sister and compassionate support from a friend. These enigmatic emotions have the potential to change lives completely; hence we can rightly conclude that sharing love is one of the most important ingredients of life. Without love life is empty, and with it, life vibrates with meaning and warmth.

If it were not for sharing love, you would not be in the world. If your grandparents were not in love, your parents would not be in the world, and if your parents were not in love, you would not be in this world. Babies can be conceived without love as well. It is sex that produces a baby, but sex does not nurture it. Love helps nurture a baby and guarantees its wellbeing and survival.

The wellbeing of humans has even proved it. If it weren't for love, people would have been sick, not only physically but mentally and emotionally as well. Children deprived of love tend to be depressed and develop cognitive, physiological and emotional impairments such as thinking difficulties, banging sensation in the head and demoralized sense of self.

To love someone and be loved by someone is one of the most essential ingredients of human survival, for nothing is more supreme in the world than the feeling of love and affection. We are born out of love, and throughout our life, maintain relationships of love with parents, siblings, friends, elders, spouse, children and so on, and it is through these relationships that we sustain a living. All through our lives, we work our way to love others and be loved by others.

For me, social love sharing is spiritual to living beings. Children need to learn how to make friends; adolescents need to learn how to interact with the opposite sex and adults must learn how to effectively relate to mates and peers.

Life without love is next to mere existence, for love is what makes life worth living. Love acts as a catalyst and allows the wheel of life to continue turning. When we are struck by love, we look at people beyond ourselves and things beyond our needs and concerns. If it weren't for love, there wouldn't have been the emotion of care, warmth, affection, concern for life.

If it weren't for love, there would be no self-esteem and no sense of self-worth. In day to day living it is love that enhances the daily living and makes life pleasurable and beautiful. People who have never experienced love in their life are often seen to hold an aggressive, hostile and emotional nature than those who have. Also, when love is there, a person can face any appalling situation financially, emotionally or physiologically and come out of it effectively. Mostly it is seen when a person has the loving support of friends, family, associates; they can then withstand any hazardous situation and emerge out as a winner.

Imagine a world without love. Well, there would be no world at all, for war and violence would have taken care of it all. Love helps maintain peace and prosperity and thus ensures living. It attaches people with the peaceful sentiment and gets rid of negative emotions like violence, aggression, brutality and hostility. It is only when people are not surrounded by love in their life that they turn hostile.

Spiritual love

Spiritual love enhances your cushion of love by trusting in something larger than yourself.

On the spiritual path, we fall short many times. It is easy to become impatient, frustrated and overwhelmed. That is why love is so important.

Love sees life in everything. It recognizes the life that abides within every creature. This recognition begets respect. Love is patient, kind and endures all things; our knowledge, plans, and strategies will reach their wits' end, but love never tires.

Love is wild and has no manners; it comforts the afflicted and afflicts the comfortable. Love often defies logic. It would have us embrace our enemies and be uncomfortably honest with our friends. This cannot be taught. Love does not come with a manual. It is the spontaneous expression of our true nature.

Love is complete and total freedom because it is selfless. Self-centeredness is the worst kind of prison. It keeps us chained and shackled to our fears and illusions, reserved to making decisions that serve our own narrow-minded agenda. Love doesn't see the world or the people in it through the knowledge of good and bad. Love does not see what we stand to lose or gain. It sees things as they are and when you see things as they are, you see the spark of divinity that lives within all things.

Everyone agrees that being "in love" is one of the most wonderful experiences life has to offer. When we are in love, every part of life shines a little brighter. Our bodies and minds tingle with energy, concerns shrivel and disappear, challenges are easily handled, and priorities fall into place with love firmly on top. Best of all, we enjoy a close and unbroken connection with our loved ones, whether the loved ones are physically with us or apart.

Fortunately, being in love is an experience we can enjoy every day of our lives. That's because the state we call being "in love" is simply a peek preview of an authentic spiritual experience. The experience of true human relationships can, and ultimately will, become our permanent realization. Most people tend to forget that the primary cause of friendships and relationships is in the mind. As a result, we tend to rely too much on physical interaction, including every form of physical closeness. We demand "live with me" and then I will know that our relationship is real, "buy me a car" and then I will know that our love is true. As if bodily togetherness was the most important ingredient in the establishment and maintenance of friendship and relationships.

There is nothing inherently wrong with symbolic physical arrangements. There certainly is some value, perhaps even a thrill, in being together physically, but we may as well admit, there is nothing cosmically fulfilling about such arrangements either. Most of all it is crucially important to realize that such arrangements cannot possibly ensure relationships, or true closeness.

We are already and eternally in sacred and beautiful friendships and relationships with each other, but we will deny and avoid the acknowledgment and realization of those friendships and relationships as long as we hold them negatively in our minds. Only by cultivating real friendships through consciously positive connection can we realize the joys of true love, and ultimately, the mystical reality of spiritual unity.

Love, friendships and relationships are like the seed of a beautiful flower. We can neglect or mishandle that seed, in which case we will never enjoy the glory of the plant in full bloom. Or we can take that seed, water it, feed it and care for it until that seed becomes a beautiful scent. The love-response is cultivated in the same dimension, in the mind and heart. This is the truth of sharing and experiencing the love-response. And this is the way to be in love forever.

Gratitude

In the embrace of unconditional love, it feels like we are loved into being. This awareness brings about a phase change. It transmutes the energy of unconditional love into gratitude. Dominion is not control but responsibility. When you are grateful for something, you tend to it.

Gratitude is an action, not an idea. It is the act of caring for that for which we are grateful. Gratitude doesn't hang out in the oceanic presence of unconditional love. It reaches out from the deep space of love. It invests not only in the maintenance of our self but through likeness, recognizes and welcomes the true self in others. Likeness is a quality of basic sanity. It looks beyond race, religion, gender, sexual orientation and social status to find its kind in others. In this way, likeness gives rise to kindness, which is the foundation of relationships. Having established relationships, love goes through yet another conversion.

Creative love

At this stage, gratitude and kindness give way to the creative power of love. It is the creative force that seeks to express love through relationships, art, poetry, music, prayers of devotion and songs. While creative love is the principle that underlies the great work of art, it is not limited to painting, music or theater any more than it is to the bedroom. In fact, creative love is more active in our daily life. It is the aspect of love that expands the field or practice. It brings our spiritual practice out of our home and into our day.

Love in daily life

It is the art of living when we consent to the power of love; it shapes our lives. This happens in relationships. We cannot wall ourselves off from the world and call it spirituality. Without relationships our practice is incomplete – commitment connects the responsibilities and obligations of our daily life to the indwelling reality of our true self.

Committed relationships are difficult because they demand that we give our self. This is hard because the false-self is selfish; it wants to avoid discomfort and clings to immediate gratification. Creative love matures us by reminding us that we cannot hope to grow into our true self without something demanding our false-self return.

Love is free to accept this maxim. This is the power of love to endure all things: marriage, divorce, success, failure, friendship, rivalries, heartache and death. The freedom of love enables us to adapt to life's changing circumstances. From the point of view of creative love, there are no problems, only opportunities. Creative love sees everything as workable.

Turning off fear

Each individual is unique, so the process of turning off fear is going to be different for each individual. One of the first steps lies in being willing to at least entertain the idea that there is something bigger that you can trust to guide your life. As long as you don't trust anything other than your cognitive mind, you are likely to feel frightened.

If you take the leap of faith that allows you to turn over even a small bit of control to this thing you begin to trust, you will start collecting evidence to prove to the cognitive mind that it really is safe to step into the unknown. As it starts getting proof that it is safe, the cognitive mind relaxes, fear lessens, and something inside of you begins to open up. The cognitive mind becomes a willing servant rather than being brutal, and the small self will take its rightful position in the back seat. As you become brave enough to let fear go, you begin to let courage take the lead in your life rather than being at fear's mercy.

It is important to understand that making this shift doesn't eliminate fear. It would be unrealistic to think you would never have a false fear thought again. The process of letting fear free you and letting courses take charge is not for the fainthearted. You are going to be asked to face the truth about who you are and who you are not.

Most of us are so blinded by self-deception that we don't even know what is true anymore. We may sense the truth, but it is often uncomfortable to face it head-on. The truth can be both brutal and wonderful. It requires examining all the limiting beliefs that are operating our lives unconsciously, and when we realize how we are creating our own suffering, it can be painful. Your fear may even rear up before it quiets down, because once you take the blinders off and illuminate all that is untrue in your life you will be more conscious of how false fear may be ruling your life. This realization may be supremely uncomfortable. Remember, any fear that gets unearthed is just more fodder for growth. Don't get frustrated, just keep returning to gratitude.

What would you do if you weren't afraid? What leaps of faith might you take? How might you love? What kinds of relationships might you have? What type of work might you do? How might you serve others? What truth would you speak? What aspects of the real you would you unveil? How would you live every aspect of your life aligned with the values of your soul? How would you feel if nothing was holding you back from living your bravest life?

Imagine this. Instead of waking up feeling afraid of what the day holds, you open your eyes feeling excited about the possibilities that lie ahead of you. You notice yourself focusing less on what you lack and more on what you appreciate. When negative emotions naturally arise, you move quickly through feelings of fear, anxiety, depression, disappointment, resentment, anger and frustration into feelings of peace, stillness and joy.

You no longer feel you have to compromise your integrity in order to get what you want. You discover greater meaning and purpose in work. You prioritize relationships with the others who are seeking to live beyond the grip of fear. The sense of disconnection, loneliness, and separation that may have plagued you gets replaced by hope hearted feelings of love, compassion, and connection with all beings. You discover an upwelling of enthusiasm for dreams, activities, and passions you have suppressed. Instead of defending against loss, you accept it is an inevitable process of initiation that grows your soul.

The small self who once chattered away in your mind frightening you with artificial doom and gloom quietens down. You sense, instead, an inner stillness that offers you refuge and makes you brave. Your new-found courage doesn't lead you to behave recklessly, because you are guided by your integrity; steered by your inner compassion, you have no need to let false fear drive your decisions and actions.

Once you make this shift, you may notice some surprising side effects. Others are magnetized by your kindness and inner calm, and you may discover that you are drawing to you people who tune to a whole different vibration.

Ten common false fear roots

1. Limiting beliefs arising from childhood, such as the belief that there is never enough to go around.
2. Generational fears, which tend to get passed down from our parents and theirs before them.
3. Memories of past dangers we have faced.
4. Projections of the fearful imagination into the future.
5. Institutional fears, such as a fear of snakes or heights, basic survival fears that all humans have to some degree.
6. Inadequate social support or mentorship.
7. Pessimistic explanatory style.
8. Fear-inducing religious upbringing.
9. Exposure and sensitivity to the excessively fear-inducing media.
10. Loss of spiritual connection.

Practicing exercises to turning off fear

1. Tonglen meditation for compassion.
2. How to turn on your intuition.
3. Be the witness.

Tonglen meditation for compassion

Tonglen, a Tibetan Buddhist practice of taking on the suffering of others and replacing it with your happiness, compassion and peace through your breath, has numerous benefits. It dissolves the self-protection, clinging and fixation of the small self and opens the heart. It reverses the small self's tendency to avoid suffering and seek pleasure and liberates you from the prison of selfishness.

In the beginning, you may find that you resist this practice. It may bring up all your revulsion, resentment, frustration, anger, and avoidance of suffering. If you experience these feelings, use them to deepen the practice. Let the poison of life's suffering become your medicine. By doing this practice, your heart will open more and more and you will become a vessel of compassion that heals others with your presence. Imagine a world in which we all practice Tonglen every day.

1. Start by cleaning your emotional landscapes. Sit quietly and focus on your breath as you allow your mind to become still. Using your breath, see yourself breathing in any negative emotions you might be feeling right now, then breathing out peace and joy. Purify your emotional landscape by repeating this process until you feel calm and clear.
2. Next, cleanse yourself. See yourself as two beings – your inner pilot light and your small self. As you breathe in, visualize your inner

pilot light breathing in all of your small self's suffering into its wide-open heart. As you breathe out, see your inner pilot light sending you small self-healing, peace, calm, love and compassion. In the compassionate embrace of your inner pilot light, your small self then responds by opening its heart too, and all of the suffering dissolves.

3. Cleanse your wrong doing by considering a situation where you didn't behave as your best self. Maybe you feel guilty or ashamed or regretful. As you think about this situation, accept responsibility for this event as you breathe in, then as you breathe out, acknowledge your wrong doing and send forgiveness to yourself and offerings of love, peace and reconciliation to the ones you harmed.

4. Now that you've cleansed your emotional landscape, your self's pain, and moved into the energy of forgiveness and reconciliation, expand your Tonglen practice for others. Start with just one person you want to help, invoke the presence of the divine into your heart, then as you feel the pain or suffering this person is feeling, visualize the pain as grimy black smoke that you breathe in. As you breathe it in, this toxic smoke dissolves in the openness of your heart and purifies your heart of any of the small self's grasping, self-

protection, or self-absorption that prevents you from sensing the oneness of all beings. As you breathe out, see yourself spreading light, love, compassion and happiness to the one brain.

5. Now expand this practice beyond one person into the collective. Breathe in the sufferings of others, then, as you breathe out, see the rays of this light, love, and compassion touching every soul on the planet. This practice can be very powerful, infusing the energy of compassion into the culture and connecting us in our web of oneness.
6. If you find yourself resisting this practice, notice any emotions that come up – resentment, fear, anger, sadness, terror, revulsion, or feelings of revenge. Also notice any physical sensations – tightness in your chest, gripping in your solar plexus, or a feeling of heaviness or darkness. As you breathe in, feel the oneness with all of the other people on the planet who are feeling just like you do. As you breathe out, send relief to all the suffering beings, including yourself.

How to strengthen your intuition

Intuition can be cultivated by some of the following to increase the intuition volume on that inner voice.

- **Meditate:** Messages from your intuition tend to be quiet, so spending time in silence will help you hear and interpret these messages.

- **Develop your sensory awareness:** Start noticing all that you can with your five conventional senses. Doing so can raise your sensitivity to your sixth sense.
- **Pay attention to your dreams:** When the cognitive mind is busy, it can override the intuitive right brain and the subconscious mind, the wellspring of intuition. But when you're sleeping, your cognitive mind rests and opens space for the subconscious mind to signal you in dreams.
- **Get creative:** Engaging in creative activities, such as drawing, scrapbooking, or free-flow journaling, quiets the cognitive mind and allows your intuition to speak up.
- **Consult oracle cards:** Learn to use a tarot deck or try a deck of oracle cards, such as Doreen virtue's Goddess Guidance Oracle Cards.
- **Test your hunches:** Got a feeling which horse will win at the track? Getting a sense that it will rain tomorrow even though the weather forecast says it won't? Do you just know your best friend's new guy is bad news? If you have a feeling about what might happen in the future, write down your hunches, then check them later. See how often you are right.
- **Consult your body compass:** Your intuition speaks to you through your body, and the more you cultivate somatic awareness, the more sensitive you become. If you get an uncomfortable physical feeling when you're

trying to make decisions, pay attention. Do you feel light or heavy? Got a sick feeling in your gut? Saddled with a headache or diarrhea? It could just be the result of stress response activated by false fear, but it could also be your intuition ringing loud and clear.

- **Spend time in nature:** Being in the natural world, away from technology and the cognitive mind's other temptations, can open up the kind of intuition we needed when we as a species lived outdoors and relied upon it to keep us safe from the elements, predators, and other true fear dangers.
- **Learn from the past:** Recall a negative experience from your past, ideally something fairly recent. Before this thing happened, think back to whether you got any feelings that urge you to steer clear. Maybe you got a gut feeling something wasn't right. Maybe you had a foreshadowing dream or a vision. If so, did you talk yourself out of it? Try to remember exactly how you feel. Recall as many details as possible. The more you can get in touch with the part of you that tried to warn you, the more you'll trust it next time.
- **Feel, don't think:** The mind thinks, always chattering away, arguing with itself like a crazy person. Intuition, on the other hand, feels. If you're not sure whether you're listening to your fearful mind or your trustworthy intuition, see if you can differentiate whether you're thinking or feeling.

Be the witness

When you find yourself getting mired in the emotions of loss (or any other emotions, for that matter), try this exercise, which helps you remember that you are not the avatar, getting shot at by life; you are the soul playing the video game of earth school.

If loss is causing you to suffer, notice the emotions you feel – grief, loneliness, anger, hurt, sadness, disappointment, anxiety, resentment. It's easy to mistakenly identify with these emotions as who you are. But what if instead of being the emotion, you are simply the soul who is with that emotion? What if, instead of being a sad person, you are the expanse of consciousness witnessing the part of you that feels sad?

Try the following exercise:

1. If you start to feel an emotional disturbance, such as anger, frustration, sadness or hurt, name the feeling and notice it.
2. Step back and witness the part of you that is disturbed by this feeling. The part of you that is feeling this feeling is your avatar. You are the soul who is witnessing the angry, hurting avatar.
3. Close your eyes and give yourself as much time as you need to fully witness the emotional disturbance. Let your soul offer love, compassion and comfort to the avatar part of your suffering.

Turning on happiness

Happiness is a natural human state, like hunger, boredom, alertness, anger and excitement. Happiness is not just a pleasurable sensation. When you are on a path that brings you happiness, it will guide you, perhaps in surprising ways, to more happiness.

Humans are born with the natural ability to be happy. However happy or unhappy you are now, you can be happier. Being happy is simple. Being unhappy is complicated.

Happiness teaches us that deep down we are all connected to each other, and it reminds us to enjoy that. Each day you are happy, that happiness increases the total sum of happiness in the world.

There are different types of happiness. You can be excited and be happy or calm and happy. You could be reading a book and be happy; you could be happy having an early morning walk or drinking a cup of coffee. You can be happy even though you don't look happy.

Everything we do in our lives is determined by our choices. Some people, of course, are born with advantages, but there are plenty of people who have achieved extraordinary things against the odds because they made decisions that dramatically changed their lives for the better. You can choose to move toward a happier life right now. One of the keys to happiness is the discovery that we can choose how to edit and direct our own lives. We are in charge of what we focus on, how we light it, how we frame it, and all other variables.

Fortunately, most people understand, at least intellectually, selfishness is the plant of a bad seed. We recognize the terrible social and personal problems caused by gross manifestations of egotism — anger, addictive attachment, neurotic aversion, etc. Unfortunately, we hardly appreciate the true depth and extent of the problem. We should strive to enjoy the freedom, unity, love and kindness we dream of.

Self-protectiveness ruins love. Stinginess limits giving. Hyper control prevents surrender. Pride cometh before the fall. Almost all achievements and joys of a sublime nature are routinely aborted by an aspect of ego. In this world, self-centered, live-for-number-one values have become the prevailing philosophies of life. Everywhere you turn, you see the blind pursuit of selfish gains. People are actually surprised and perhaps suspicious when anyone acts other than in their own self-interest.

If we are living right, we are not living for ourselves. Happiness will come as a result of right living, but only secondary effects. The rewards of right living are not our appropriate concern. Clearly, being unselfish is good for everyone, but if our main reason for being unselfish is our personal benefit, we are not being unselfish, we are being selfish. That's the paradise of right living. The fact that it's good for us can't be the primary motivation and still have it be right.

The true and rightful purpose of life is self-transcending love and unselfish service. No one can ever love or serve truly while living the life of the ego. Ego is unalterably and consistently opposed to real love and loving, and externally afraid of giving. Love and service are the reverse of the tendency to act in the name of lower self-interest and ego-survival.

Granted it is human nature to want to improve your circumstances. It is totally natural to strive to reduce your suffering, your confusion, your problems, your limitations. It is natural to increase your safety, your security, your comfort, your satisfaction, your convenience, your knowledge and pleasure.

Our natural responses are built into our genetic, physical makeup. Therefore we cannot be faulted for them. Nonetheless, a natural life of unbridled tendency consists of little more than surrender to ego. In that case, ego tells us what we can do and what we are not allowed to do. And what can be channeled through is obstructed.

You, as you (mis)understand yourself to be, stand in the way of happiness acting through you freely. Therefore, until and unless you allow ego to be undone in you, you are simply, though perhaps unconsciously, preventing the flow of divine impulse into life. When it comes down to the actual choice points of existence, you should transcend what is merely natural in order to become a kind, loving person.

Turning on true love and happiness is not an easy way. The pearl of great price was never meant to be cheap. It is costly, at times painful, but whatever its price may be, the rewards infinitely outweigh it. Miserable self-denial is simply ego's opinion of happiness; it is an utter falsification of the life divine. Think about the most ecstatic moments of your life, every one of them was an experience of self-transcendence.

True freedom is not freedom to do whatever we want; true freedom is freedom from what we, as egos, want. It is liberation from ego, no less! When ego is released, the problem of self-resolve into the realization of self becomes our divine reality.

What does happiness Look like?

- Happiness Looks very radiant.
- Happiness Looks and feels like you are in heaven.
- Happiness Looks and feels like you are connected to the beloved.
- Happiness Looks like a beautiful rose in a flower garden.
- Happiness Looks like a gorgeous smile.
- Happiness Looks like a signpost which leads to a brighter future.
- Happiness Looks like a key that opens doors for success.
- Happiness Looks like a heart full of love that keeps you going.

Labels

In our society, we give people labels too easily. And if it is repeated enough, people put it on as an identity and build stories to support it. Some labels are positive, like "I am a true friend," but others are negative, like "I am not sociable." While there may be some truth in these stories some of the time, the more we tell ourselves these stories, the more we believe them to be permanent. They are all just stories, some of them support us, and some of them don't, but they can be changed.

Elvis Presley, Richard Branson, Michael Jordan and Einstein were all told "nothing will ever become of you." If these people had accepted those labels they would not have become world famous and successful.

Sometimes we hear negative labels so much we begin to use it ourselves. As we hear more and more labels we weave them into the story we tell ourselves. Here are some of the things we tell ourselves:

- I feel like I am not meant to be happy.
- We are all depressives in my family.
- It is not worth trying to feel good because it will make me feel worse.
- The things I have experienced mean I can never be truly happy.
- I have always felt like I don't fit in.

- Whatever I do, it won't make any difference.
- My worries are far too real; I can't ignore them.

What we don't realize is that these stories that we keep telling ourselves are the beliefs that hold us back from the changes we want to make.

Some parts of these stories are nourishing and empowering, and some parts of the stories bring us down.

Happiness is not the same as pleasure. Pleasure is wonderful, and a lot of people are all in favor of it. We can get pleasure from all sorts of aspects of life. It is great to enjoy a hot bath, view the beautiful sunset, enjoy our favorite meal. But pleasure on its own will not make you happy. If you do one pleasurable thing after another eventually you will get bored. There is only so much candy you can eat. You would even get bored of French fries if that's what you mostly ate. If you only do things for pleasure, however fine or expensive, sooner or later you will be left feeling is this all there is?

If happiness were determined by pleasure, then the people with the most money would be the happiest people. Rich people in first world countries are no happier than tribes are in Africa.

Happiness includes pleasure, but it is different. Happiness is something deeper. Happiness is a backdrop to your life which makes everyday life rewarding; it gives you strength in hard times, and it frees you to enjoy life fully at every opportunity.

The reason happiness seems difficult to define is that it is unique to each individual. There is no one thing or event that would make any person happy all the time. Happiness arises from respecting your own highest values and deepest wishes.

It is easy to look at other people and other situations and imagine that we would be happy if we had what they had. But remember, the key to happiness is not what you have but how good you are at appreciating it.

Don't compare the outside of someone else with the inside of you.

Friendship and happiness

Friendship is such a rich source of happiness. When we are with friends who are warm and appreciative, it feels good. We all like to be loved and appreciated; Mother Teresa said, "There is more hunger for love and appreciation in this world than for bread."

At another level, we increase our happiness by sharing our happiness. Putting a smile on someone's face rewards the deep sense of community that is hard-wired into us. Being kind or polite creates a sense of good community, which is why we can feel good performing any act of kindness, whether to a close friend or to a stranger.

Some people are a bit wary of being too kind because they fear someone might take advantage of them. It doesn't cost anything to pay a compliment or to smile.

Sometimes just a smile makes all the difference. We are influenced by non-verbal signals all the time, so we can't help feeling better every time we experience genuine kindness. That's why good things happen to you when you are happy. When you feel good, the world looks good.

The essence of friendship is not grand gestures but kindness and caring. So being a friend does not mean helping everyone all the time or endlessly buying gifts. It means small expressions of appreciation in everyday contexts.

Happiness is a great creator of friendship; happy people make friends easily. Some people have lots of friends, and some people are really happy with very few friends. Like attracts like, so happy people gather happy friends.

When you are happy with yourself, someone else is more able to be happy with you. The basis of good friendships is a good relationship with yourself.

We can see this is true if we imagine the situation from the point of view of your partner. If you are not at ease with yourself, you will be edgy and difficult to live with. So to relate well to others, you should relate well to yourself, so when you think of yourself, you have a positive and accepting attitude. At the same time, you must be kind and sensitive enough to accept and respect your own vulnerabilities.

As you are happy in yourself, there will be no hidden agenda in your relationships. You won't be trying to get other people to make you happy, you already are.

Part Three

The Love-Response Helper

The healing process

Recovering from abuse, social isolation, fear and so on does not happen overnight, it is an ongoing process. It involves feeling a lot of pain along the way, allowing a healing process to start within you. Healing starts with expecting more from yourself. No individual is under obligation to keep lining themselves up to be abused, belittled and humiliated.

Don't be harsh on yourself. You will never love yourself enough to change your expectations if you keep flogging yourself for not being strong enough. You are a child of the universe who deserves to be happy.

No verbal, emotional, physical abuse or neglect is healthy for a human's brain. The human brain is incredibly adaptive, and in response to an abusive environment it will shut down to protect itself as much as it can from the abuse. It can make a person vulnerable to the reduction of immunity, reduce resilience to stress, cognitive impairment, anxiety and so on.

Steps you can take

Here are a few steps you can take to find joy, love and inner strength:

- Keep reminding yourself that these unpleasant days will be over one day, and better days are coming.
- Take responsibility for seeing yourself as a valuable person.
- Start volunteer work to increase your social friendships.
- Stop believing that you are useless.
- Take a leap of faith and follow your passion to work really hard and gain success, love, and happiness.
- Stop feeling insecure, blaming and judging other people.
- Learn to forgive.
- Listen to the positive inner voice inside you; it will give you a real lift in confidence.
- Learn to identify positive and negative emotional wellbeing.

The 11/11 healing for healing self

How the 11/11 healing process can help

This process is a powerful method, over time, for changing a false belief system that isn't serving you into a positive belief system. The numbers 11/11 are known by spiritualists as a portal of manifestation. Many people attest to seeing the numbers 11/11 continually in everyday life, such as clocks, license plates and signs.

Individuals who have worked with this process diligently and correctly have indeed experienced great shifts in thinking and behavior as well as created powerful positive manifestations.

The 11/11 process works when a person establishes an essential and intimate relationship with themselves. Your conscious mind is focusing upon a new positive program and filtering this to your subconscious; false belief systems will be released from your subconscious to make space for the new positive program.

What can be expected from doing the 11/11 healing process?

People and situations will reflect back to you; your new internal belief system, for example, "I love and accept myself" will start creating outer conditions that support this belief. As a result of working with the process, you will feel peace, empowerment and a greater connection with yourself. Your response will contain vital information as to which belief systems will require ongoing reprograming. Your subconscious will reveal the next steps in your healing journey. Your thoughts, words and actions will start supporting your new belief system, which powerfully assists the creation of the life you wish to live.

How to do the 11/11 healing process

Write the positive belief system down in a journal. As you do so, focus on the positive statement. After writing this statement, sit and wait for your mind to grant a response. Do not judge the response in any way, simply write it. It could be anything ranging from negativity/disbelief to positivity/belief or any related issues or any unrelated issues. If nothing comes to mind write "no response." The response can be as long or as short as you wish.

Continue this process 11 times.

Do this process once a day for 11 days straight.

The full 11 positive statements and responses must be written in one sitting with no breaks or distractions.

An example of the 11/11 healing process

Journal entries: day 1

1	Affirmation:	I unconditionally love and accept myself.
	Response:	I don't know if I can do this. This feels so hard. Part of me is sitting here saying "what the hell – what do I need to do this for?" Another part of me really knows that for some reason I have to. I can't even imagine having a conversation like this with myself. Normally I would sit down, tune out and watch TV.

2	Affirmation:	I unconditionally love and accept myself.
	Response:	So here I am doing this – okay, what is it going to mean? What does loving me feel like? It certainly has to feel better than the horrible versions of love I've had. What is love anyway? If it means feeling better and really being able to trust someone again and open my heart, I guess it's got to be okay. Anything's got to be better than what's happened before.
3	Affirmation:	I unconditionally love and accept myself.
	Response:	So I'm doing really well – up to the third one already, and I haven't walked away yet, wow, I'm good. How interesting! How often do I cover up my feelings with humor – now I am uncomfortable having a conversation with myself, especially one that is about telling myself something nice. Come to think of it, it's always been hard for me to accept any compliments from anyone.
4	Affirmation:	I unconditionally love and accept myself.
	Response:	Who am I trying to kid? I don't love myself, I never have. If I loved

myself, I wouldn't drink myself into oblivion every chance I have, and I wouldn't keep choosing men who beat the crap out of me. It's really pretty obvious that I have terrible self-worth and self-love. I am sick to death of proving how tough I am and putting on a front. The bottom line is I am terrified of getting hurt and damaged again – and then I shortcut the system by damaging myself first.

5 Affirmation: I unconditionally love and accept myself.

Response: So I know I am supposed to be really honest with my responses, and I am really trying to. What on earth else can I say? Alright, you want to know the truth? Of course, I'd love to believe this statement, who wouldn't? It's been so hard trying to feel alright. Why on earth couldn't I have grown up feeling loved? Why did I have to go through what I did? Of course, I know the reason why – to heal myself. But it still hurts. Great, I am crying now – as if I need more pain.

6 Affirmation: I unconditionally love and accept myself.

Response: I know, I know – get it out! So I am really focusing on this statement "I love myself," I am trying. I want this. I want so badly to feel loved, safe and protected. I never have been. I've never felt this, ever in my whole life. Please, someone, help me, help me feel this one day. Okay, breathe. I know I am going to be okay. It's perfectly alright to feel this pain – surely what isn't going to kill me is going to make me stronger.

7 Affirmation: I unconditionally love and accept myself.

Response: So what are the choices – throw in the towel because I am crying and go and pick up a drink or stay here with my journal? I am sick of giving into myself and causing more pain – okay, no matter what it takes I am determined. I am sick of my life, and I want to change it for the better. I am 43 years of age and feel like I have never gotten anywhere. It's time I did something about it. I really do know no one is ever going to love me unless I learn to love myself.

8 Affirmation: I unconditionally love and accept myself.

Response: Okay journal, I am here with you. Whew! That feels better; I was nearly tempted for a moment. No more crap! What a rollercoaster – all because I am sitting here writing to myself telling me "I love myself," – is it any wonder I never believed anybody else who said these words? Is it any wonder that I viewed them with suspicion or was waiting for them to leave, hurt me, or run off with another woman, just like my father did?

9 Affirmation: I unconditionally love and accept myself.

Response: What a bloody system. What if I don't want to be me? What if God got it wrong? Do I get a trade-in or a refund? Can't I swap bodies with someone else, someone who's got fewer wrinkles?

10 Affirmation: I unconditionally love and accept myself.

Response: That was pretty funny. Now I am laughing, sugar! I really do take it all way too seriously. So what if I have a few wrinkles? I don't expect other people to be perfect, so why on earth do I think I have to be? Even good-looking movie stars have wrinkles. Wrinkles have never made someone sad.

11 Affirmation: I unconditionally love and accept myself.

Response: I know I can do this. So there really is a lot to love about me when I think about it. There are plenty of people that appreciate me. The problem is I have been too busy hooking into the people that don't and trying to make them accept me. I would do much better by simply loving me and allowing other loving people to be around me.

This process continues each day for 11 days straight.

Journal entries: day 5

1 Affirmation: I unconditionally love and accept myself.

Response: I am pretty proud of myself. I did the best grocery shopping I can remember doing in a long time. I actually feel like cooking for myself again. I can't believe it! Surely this must mean I am starting to love myself. Everyone at work has commented by saying how much better I look. Sure, it only took four nights of balling my eyes out – but hey it must have been worth it.

2 Affirmation: I unconditionally love and accept myself.

Response: So here we go again. I have been such a good girl. I haven't had a drink one night since I have started doing this. I am probably too scared of what I'll write if I am drunk. Actually, I know I won't do it if I start drinking and I am determined to go through with this. I really have to admit I am feeling better already.

3 Affirmation: I unconditionally love and accept myself.

Response: So, dear journal, I am spending more time with you having conversations than I can remember being bothered to talk to anyone for a long time. But this having conversations with myself — surely people get locked up for doing this! I must say I have been sleeping so much better than I can remember for a long time. I am not feeling anywhere near as lonely as I was, and I really am not tempted to get back together with that loser. Thank God!

Partial examples of day 11

1 Affirmation: I unconditionally love and accept myself.

Response: I can feel me coming on! Yes! I got a pay rise today, and my brother has invited me to Queensland for a week, and he has offered to pay. This is pretty good. Life truly isn't that bad after all, and I still haven't had a drink. I really don't feel like it.

2 Affirmation: I unconditionally love and accept myself.

Response: A couple of guys told me how cool I look! Not that I am interested in any of them, but it is really nice to get the compliments. I certainly haven't felt like I could bother feeling attractive. Now I want to go out and get a new wardrobe or at least some bits and pieces – money permitting.

3 Affirmation: I unconditionally love and accept myself.

Response: I know this is working. I can feel it. My life really is pretty good. I do have a lot to be thankful for. When I think of what some people have to try to deal with, I really do have it pretty good. I know now I have a focus on myself and am feeling better. And I have stopped drinking. I'm nowhere near as unhappy and stressed as I used to be. I really want to find a hobby now. I used to play tennis years ago, and I loved it. I wonder if Anne would like to join something with me, she used to play when she was younger too.

Continue through to number 11.

Mindfulness with love-response

Mindfulness skills are central to love-response techniques. Mindfulness has to do with the quality of awareness that a person brings to everyday living.

Mindfulness practice is the intentional process of observing, describing and participating in reality non-judgmentally in the moment with effectiveness. Mindfulness skills can also be thought of as the healing components that together make up the foundation for meditation practices taught in many psychological and stress treatment programs. Example: mindfulness-based cognitive therapy, mindfulness-based stress reduction. Mindfulness-based approaches are intended to teach people practical skills that can help with daily and ongoing life challenges, physical and psychological health problems.

What is mindfulness?

Mindfulness is simply the practice of being aware of present moment internal and external experience without trying to push it away or to overengage with what is happening. Mindfulness helps train the mind to pay attention and notice so that action can be taken with greater reflection and control. It has moved from a largely obscure Buddhist concept to a mainstream psychotherapy construct in recent years. This is probably due to the benefits that mindfulness can deliver, if well practiced, including self-control, objectivity, tolerance, enhanced flexibility, equanimity, improved concentration and mental clarity, emotional intelligence and the ability to relate to others and one's self with kindness, acceptance and compassion. *(David and Hayer, 2011)*

Benefits of integrating mindfulness with love-response

- Helps you become fully engaged in activities and creates a greater capacity to deal with hurtful events.
- By focusing on the here and now you will be less likely to get caught up in worrying about finding love and happiness in the future and overcome your past hurt.
- Supports positive attitude that contributes to a satisfied and happy life.
- Improves wellbeing.

- Helps promote empathy.
- Improves energy levels.
- Improves your personal and social relationships.
- Reduces hostility and conflicts with peers.
- Increases self-esteem,
- Increases feelings of happiness and wellbeing.
- Acts as a means of prevention against bullying, as well as a method of coping.

Mindfulness, when integrated with love-response, can improve your mental health by helping with:

- Depression.
- Substance abuse.
- Eating disorders.
- Couple conflicts.
- Anxiety.
- Obsessive-compulsive disorder.
- Improving concentration.
- Turning off the negative self-talk that our mind often resorts to when left on our own.
- Forgiving and showing empathy toward others.
- Enjoying the world around us and understanding ourselves better.
- Lessening fear and loneliness.
- Improving resilience against hurt and adversity.

- Developing social connections.
- Improving your mood and emotional intelligence.
- Better decision making and cognitive skills.
- Lessening brain problems by increasing the awareness of your unconscious mind.

Many experts believe that mindfulness works, in part, by helping people to accept their experiences, including painful emotions, rather than react to them with aversion and avoidance.

Mindfulness and love-response improve a person's mental health by:

- Relieving stress.
- Lowering blood pressure.
- Reducing chronic pain.
- Improving sleep.
- Alleviating gastrointestinal difficulties.
- Increasing your immune functions.
- Decreasing inflammatory disorders.
- Decreasing cellular level inflammation.
- Helping to treat premenstrual and menopausal symptoms.

Mindfulness formal and informal practices

The seven attitudes of mindfulness
– Jon Kabat-Zinn

Jon Kabat-Zinn is an American Professor of Medicine emeritus and the creator for mindfulness in medicine, health care and the society at the University of Massachusetts Medical School.

Jon Kabat-Zinn (1990) described attitudinal qualities that underpin mindfulness practice, which are both the stance we bring to the practice and a consequence of it. These qualities are brought to the heart of the interaction between teacher and participant in a mindfulness session. The qualities are listed below:

- Non-judging.
- Patience.
- Beginner's mind.
- Trust.
- Non-striving.
- Acceptance.
- Letting go.

Seven attitudes of mindfulness meditation
– Jon Kabat-Zinn

1. Non-judgment: impartial witnessing, observing your evaluations and categorizations.
    - Noticing the automatic habit of labeling everything we experience as good, bad or neutral.

- The habit of judging locks us into mechanical reactions that we are not even aware of and often has little objective basis.
- By becoming aware of your judgments, you can choose actions and behaviors more consciously rather than automatically reacting to situations in your environment.

The principle will be useful as you start to engage in new mindfulness practices that your mind may judge as boring or a waste of time.

2. Patience: allowing things to unfold in their time, bringing patience to ourselves and others.
    - This is an understanding that sometimes things must unfold in their own time.
    - This principle reminds you to be patient with yourself as your mind is stretched in new ways.

Patience is a helpful quality to invoke when the mind is agitated. To be patient is to be open to each moment as it unfolds knowing that, like the butterfly, some things can only unfold in their own time. So when starting out your mindfulness practice or anything else, please stick through whatever takes place trusting that some things will make more sense after you have practiced them for a while.

3. Beginner's mind: willing to see things as if for the first time.
    - We let our beliefs about a situation prevent us from seeing things as they really are.

- No moment is the same as any other.
- Beginner's mind allows us to be receptive to new possibilities and prevents us from getting stuck in our mind, which often thinks it knows more than it does.

Try to cultivate your own beginner's mind as an experiment. The next time you see someone familiar, notice if you are seeing the person with fresh eyes or through the lens of your beliefs about that person. If you encounter a new activity, notice if you are open to trying it out fully or have you already decided before doing it that you don't like it? When you are out walking, see if you are noticing things that you had overlooked before. Developing beginner's mind opens you to possibilities in life you may be missing out on because you are viewing everything through the lens shaped by past experience that is not aware of what else there is to learn and explore.

4. Trust: developing trust in your feelings and yourself is an integral part of the mindfulness practice.
    - The act of trusting yourself and your basic wisdom is an important aspect of the mindfulness training.
    - If you are feeling strongly about something it is important to attend to that rather than ignore it because an outside authority is telling you to do so.
    - Mindfulness is an objective process of inquiry, and accepting what people of

"authority" tell you without questioning the validity of it yourself is against the basic premise of mindfulness.

- It is important to stay open and learn from other sources, but ultimately you have to live your life and make the choices that feel right for you.

It is almost easier to trust external authorities to tell us how to live our lives. Mindfulness involves practicing trusting your own feelings, and that doesn't mean you react based upon all your feelings but that you explore any feelings that show up fully to see what they are telling you about a situation, and then you trust yourself to come up with the right action.

5. Non-striving: non-goal orientated, remaining unattached to outcome or achievement.

- Even though everyone undertaking mindfulness practice has some goals and intentions while they are taking their training, at the time of mindfulness practice itself, simply do the practice without any expectation.
- When you set expectations such as feeling more relaxed, you are introducing conditions that don't allow you to be fully present with what is, because you are trying to change the present to be sometime else. If you are trying to change the present, then you are not being with what is, which is what mindfulness training is.

- Remember to allow anything and everything that you experience from moment to moment to be there, because it already is. If you are tensed, just pay attention to the tension. If you are criticizing yourself, just observe the activity of the judging mind.

Non-striving may be the most difficult of all the principles because in our culture we are taught to be goal-orientated and to be constantly doing something in order to reach our goals. In mindfulness, you will reach your goals by not trying to change the present but by being present to whatever arises, and in that way, you will find that the goals are ultimately reached. This is perhaps something you will need to experience for yourself to really understand.

6. Acceptance: open to seeing and acknowledging things as they are. It does not mean approval or resignation.

- Acceptance is the willingness to see things as they really are.
- Acceptance does not mean that you have to be satisfied with the way things are or that you don't do anything to change what you don't like.
- When you have the ability to see things as they are you free up energy to take the appropriate actions of working with the mind that is clouded by denial, prejudices, fears and self-judgments.

7. Letting go: non-attachment and the ability to put aside the tendency to elevate some aspects of our experience and to reject others.
    - Letting go is a way of letting things be, of accepting things as they are.
    - When you observe your mind grasping or pushing away, you can remind yourself to let go of the impulse to grasp or push away and see what happens.
    - If you can't let go, try the opposite, of really holding on and seeing what that feels like. By looking at how you hold on, you will learn how to let go.
    - Letting go is something you naturally do when you sleep. If you have trouble sleeping, then it could be because you are not able to let go.

The following is a mindfulness meditation you can practice regularly.

Mind wide open – (The Learning State).

'With your eyes remaining open gently assume a comfortable seating position, still keeping your eyes open, allow your awareness to be with your breathing… Not trying to change your breathing at all but simply being aware… Of course, we are not normally aware of our breathing until someone draws our attention to it… We just take it for granted – do we not?

Wherever you are looking now and without moving your head, just allow your focus to soften... And both inwardly and outwardly let your visual awareness extend a little above you... And then a little more and then as high as you comfortably can without straining or getting any discomfort in your eyes... Then let your awareness extend downward in the same way, comfortably and easily... And then the same to your left, and then to your right...

With a real sense of curiosity, notice just how far you can see all around you... Gently and easily and with a feeling of comfort simply allow yourself to begin opening up a state of calm alertness... Not forcing this at all, but simply noticing how unwanted thoughts can float away like clouds on a summer's day while you become more and more aware of how your mind can be open and receptive to new learning... And now you can just allow your eyes to gently close.'

The breathing space (Hour Glass).

Expansive awareness

Notice what you are feeling at this moment physically and emotionally... What do you notice about your posture and how your posture feels? Do you feel particularly comfortable in any way and if so where is this?... Be curious about what thoughts you are aware of going through your mind at this moment... can you place a little distance between you and your thoughts? Try to observe them non-judgmentally and in a detached way, rather than being caught up in them.

Narrowing into breathing

Narrow your attention now to inside yourself and into your own breathing... Bring your attention down to your breathing and the gentle rise and fall of your abdomen. You're not trying to change your breathing in any way... just simply being aware of it in a friendly open way. It will, of course, be quite natural for your attention to wander away from your breathing and if this happens, just notice where your attention has gone and then gently lead it back to your breathing again.

Expanding awareness

Allow your conscious awareness to expand once again... from your abdomen and into your whole body. If you can, notice a feeling of breathing into your whole body. As it happens, your whole body does breathe, through your skin. See if you can be aware of a sense of wholeness and completeness in yourself... fully accepting and non-striving... Okay to be just who you are at this moment.

Gently open your eyes and have a stretch.

Attitudes to happiness

In teaching mindfulness, it may be useful to explore your client's attitude to that very elusive thing – happiness. So often if we ask someone "are you happy?" it may be something that they will automatically answer yes to, but sometimes the way they say yes won't fill you with confidence that this is what they really mean! Occasionally their body language and their words may be out of congruence. Perhaps a slight, almost imperceptible shake of their head to accompany the yes response!

Happiness may be thought of as "if only I had this or that, I would be happy." None of us are immune to this line of thought, and we all know that the achievement of "whatever it is" will rarely lead to true happiness. It is much more elusive than that and so much more to do with what is going on inside than what is going on outside. In positive psychology, the achievement of happiness is described in three different ways. All three can be combined for best effect.

The attainment of pleasure

Doing anything that we enjoy can lead us to pleasure/happiness. If you really enjoy tasty and spicy food, then going out for a meal with a close friend to a favorite Oriental or Indian restaurant may do it for you. The anticipation of doing it, to looking forward to it, may also create happiness, so long as it's not too long to wait.

Flow state

When we are fully engaged in an activity and giving it our 100% attention, then it is likely that we are in what might be described as a flow state. I used to do a lot of running, and there is something about running that means that after you have kept going and you have broken through the pain threshold, eventually you enter a state where you feel you can just keep on running (a Forrest Gump moment)! When we achieve this, we sometimes feel as if life has slowed down and we are on automatic pilot. Runners will often talk about "runner's high" to describe the euphoric feelings associated with being in this state.

Other activities requiring either intense physical activity or an intense concentration will result in similar flow or zone states. When we are in the flow we typically may experience:

- A sense of blissful awareness.
- A complete and exclusive focus.
- A sense of being at one with the universe.
- A forgetting or release of unwanted feelings and thoughts.
- A sense of inner satisfaction.

Ironically you may not notice your happiness at the time because you are in the flow!

Engaging in meaningful activities

For some people happiness seems to elude them even though they have apparently successful lives and what most people might think of as an abundance of prosperity, good health and fulfilling relationships e.g. a loving family. Could it be that the missing piece of their happiness puzzle is about giving in some way, or a feeling of wanting to be more than who they think they are? Perhaps they feel lacking in identity or purpose in their lives. The answer may be in giving some of their time – being involved in a scheme that will help others – perhaps just giving more to their family. It may be that a feeling of not belonging can be satisfied by having a religious faith.

Mindfulness teaching methodologies

Teaching and practitioners of mindfulness require teaching skills. In my view, it is all teaching, and I take the same view of therapy. Therapists are teachers and should be teaching their clients, as much as doing things to them, so that eventually the client can become their own therapist.

Therapeutic (clinical) interventions with mindfulness

Not strictly regarded as a therapy, there can be doubt and indeed there is a wealth of scientific evidence that mindfulness, in a clinical sense, is very valuable and a powerful way of achieving/enhancing health and wellbeing.

The absolute joy of offering clinical mindfulness is that clients view it as something which is non-threatening, where they don't have to reveal their innermost thoughts, where they don't have to recall and relive painful, traumatic memories, and which is simple to learn and practice at home. Clients invariably find the process enjoyable and very enlightening – a fresh way of looking at things.

Fortunately, mindfulness can be readily integrated with other therapeutic modalities. For example, person-centered counseling lends itself well to support the philosophy of the being mode rather than the doing mode, and person-centered counseling clients are encouraged to talk about their experiences without being self-critical, without judging and with an attitude of open curiosity. Stress management coaches and consultants find that they can readily integrate mindfulness into their programs, especially those aimed at developing resilience. The Mindfulness-Based Stress Reduction program and adaptations of it can be taught if there is sufficient time within stress management programs.

Mindfulness-Based Stress Reduction (MBSR)

The Mindfulness-Based Stress Reduction (MBSR) was developed in 1979 by Dr. Jon Kabat-Zinn and colleagues at the University of Massachusetts. MBSR was a pioneering integration of mindfulness meditation practices into an accessible and proactive eight-session program with psycho-educational support. At the time this was a major breakthrough from psychological/ medical models of treating stress and it has received very wide enthusiastic support and is increasingly adopted into mainstream medical approaches worldwide.

Originally taught to groups of patients with a range of physical and psychological conditions including stress, anxiety and pain, this has now been adapted and widened to include a wide variety of conditions including cancer, rheumatism, addictions and eating disorders.

Mindfulness-Based Cognitive Therapy (MBCT)

Mindfulness-Based Cognitive Therapy (MBCT) was developed by Dr. Mark Williams and colleagues at the University of Oxford, Oxford Mindfulness Centre, which offers highly respected academics learning programs. MBCT builds upon the MBSR programs to offer an evidence-based approach to helping people, particularly people with a history of depression. Such people are vulnerable to relapse, and the MBCT program can help them to be aware of bodily sensations, thoughts and feelings and then to make an adaptive response to the early signs of recurring depression.

The MBCT program has, at its core, the application of mindfulness along with key elements of MBSR and cognitive behavioral therapy (CBT) approaches. An MBCT program normally contains:

- The development/learning of awareness — achieved through mindfulness practice.
- The learning of appropriate attitudinal frameworks which includes acceptance, non-striving, and seeing with beginner's eyes.
- The cultivating of a greater understanding of the nature of vulnerability and in particular vulnerability to depressive relapse.

Separate ourselves from patterns of ruminating thinking

Since the human mind is only capable of processing a limited number of pieces of information at any one time, one or two, *(George A. Miller, 1956),* if we pay attention to certain (negative) aspects of our experience, we necessarily exclude other aspects from our conscious awareness, and by doing so we may ignore positive and powerful resources that could enable us to avoid depressive relapse. If we focus on present moment awareness, and in particular our bodily and emotional feelings through mindfulness, then our attention is removed from negative, ruminative thinking.

So instead of cognitive processing in order to solve potential or perceived problems, we simply acknowledge thoughts as part of our awareness "landscape." By doing this, we can pre-empt the development of negative repeating patterns. If we continue to practice mindfulness exercises, then we begin to train our own subconscious processing to create superior and fully intentional behaviors, as opposed to the negative ones driven by automatic processing. New, more positive and resourceful patterns become "hard-wired" so as to be accessible in times of low mood, before sinking into a major depression.

How can mindfulness be an effective part of coaching?

Curiosity

As a performance coach, a good dose of curiosity can achieve wonders at times. It can be argued that one of the key skills of coaches is to be able to somehow get our clients to think and to think creatively "outside the box." That's why "grow" model option questions like "what other options do you think you have?" and "if anything were possible, what would you do?" and even perhaps when things are getting stuck, if you did not know the answer, "what would it be?" can be most helpful in developing "way forward" options.

Mindfulness can help us to develop curiosity, particularly with a kind of non-judgmental reflection. Have you noticed how, when you reflect on something that you have written, maybe your journal or notes for some forthcoming event, in a fairly quiet, distraction-free (almost meditative) state, that real inspiration can come to mind? The essence of curiosity can be found in "inquiry" type, powerful questions in coaching. The sort of questions that the answer to which may have a real impact on the coaching issue. The answer to these sort of questions, such as "how can you identify what is really holding you back?" may not immediately find an answer at a conscious level. The client may need to reflect and let it settle quietly before an answer comes to mind. The mindfulness body scan exercise can be helpful here.

Beginner's mind

One of the most quoted attitudes/principles of mindfulness is known as beginner's mind. Rather than responding to events in the way we always have before, rather than thinking and doing in the way we always have before, just supposing we were able to see things as if we were looking through a completely new pair of eyes.

Presence

Our presence in the coaching relationship may be considered as one of coaching's core competencies. Just how genuinely present are we in that relationship? What does being present mean?

Staying present really means letting go of our awareness of ourselves so that we become more aware of our client. Conversely, if we start to become more aware of ourselves within the coaching conversation, perhaps thinking about how we look, how we are sounding, letting any of our own personal thoughts intrude, then we decrease our awareness of our client. When this happens, we start to listen less effectively, and we are less likely to perceive non-verbal communication, so we are unable to check out congruence in communication. We actually become less conscious of the whole coaching process.

So presence may be thought of as something which all of us in our profession believe we have a natural aptitude for, rather like an ability to build rapport. That doesn't mean to say, however, that we can't become even more effective if we work at it.

Being truly present is actually a very joyful state to be in. When we feel we are at one in the moment but at the same time unattached to the outcome, it is as if we are somehow connected to some kind of source of inspiration. We can truly be in a state of "flow" where everything seems effortless, and where we are open to all possibilities.

Mindfulness with children

Is there anywhere that mindfulness is not becoming an important topic? In the USA and the UK, the idea of mindfulness in the classroom has really taken off. The idea of introducing the basic elements of mindfulness to children, of any age, makes very good sense indeed.

Children are of course naturally in the present, and therefore mindful. They look at everyday things with great wonder and curiosity, without judgment and with a lack of self-criticism. They tend not to have our adult habit of being preoccupied with the past and the future. Mindfulness can help children to remain with their wonderful sense of openness and can help it to grow rather than allowing it to be stifled, as can easily happen as the child matures.

Mindfulness exercises for preschool children

"Children can be introduced to the principles of mindfulness from a young age," says Roy Hintsa, a Toronto area stress reduction facilitator. Children of all ages can benefit from different styles of training. Younger children tend to respond more to physical activities rather than practicing meditation. Here are some exercises Roy recommends for preschool children:

- **Mindful listening:** tell your child you are going to ring a bell or a tone bar. Ask them to listen carefully to the sound of the bell and raise their hands when they can no longer hear it.
- **Breath awareness:** have your child lie down on a mat on the floor, or on their bed, and place their favorite stuffed animal on their belly. Have them rock the stuffed animal to sleep with the movement of their belly as they breathe in and out. This is how they can begin to pay attention to their breathing.
- **Mindful eating:** this is a time when playing with your food is okay! Give your child a piece

of fruit and ask them to imagine they are from another planet and have never seen this piece of fruit before. Ask them to describe their experience using all five senses. What does it look like? Smell like? Feel like? Taste like? Does it make a sound when you bite it?

I like the idea of integrating mindfulness with music, hence I decided to introduce mindfulness rapping/hip hop to my book.

Mindfulness rapping

Timothy Scott Jr. is a mindful hip hop artist and mindfulness instructor from California's Bay Area. Since 2012 he has been spreading love and insight on mindfulness and wellbeing. Bringing students and their families positivity, mindful practices and wellbeing, the following term has been coined "mindful hip hop."

Stress Strategies/Coping Skills

What is stress?

Stress is the feeling of being under too much mental pressure. Stress can affect how you feel, think, and how your body works.

Stress journal

A stress journal can help you identify the regular stressors in your life and the way you deal with them. Each time you feel stressed, keep track of it in your journal. As you keep daily logs, you will begin to see patterns and common themes. Write down the following:

- What causes you stress?
- Who you were with?
- How you felt emotionally and physically?
- What were you thinking?
- Avoid people who stress you out by:

    a. limiting the amount of time you spend with them

    or

    b. ending the friendship

Stress is a commonly experienced problem. You are likely to know others who have been in a similar situation. There is no need to feel embarrassed or concerned. Often it can help to tell others about how you feel. Stress is not harmful in itself. You are not weak because you struggle with it. Stress over a long period of time can, however, make us more vulnerable to health problems.

Physical feelings are experienced when your body reacts to stress, fear or anxiety. These symptoms are often referred to as the "fight or flight" response. This reaction quickly and helpfully prepares the body for action. It prepares us to either protect against or escape danger in the following ways:

- Producing more sweat – to cool us down.
- Tensing our muscles – getting them ready for action.
- Making our heart beat faster – to supply more blood to our muscles.
- Racing thoughts – quickly narrowing the available options to make a quick response.

What causes stress?

Life events: particular life events can cause people significant problems with stress. Difficulties that were previously manageable might also become much more challenging to cope with, for example:

- Divorce or family turmoil.
- Health problems.
- Being unemployed.
- Neighborhood problems.
- Financial difficulties.
- Death of a relative.

Thinking styles: stress can impact how we think about ourselves and other people. We are more likely to think negatively about a situation. You might think that what is being demanded of you outweighs your ability to manage.

Biological reasons: there may be some traits that biological factors predispose individuals to experience more stress than others. A high concentration of stress over a long period of time can weaken your immune system.

Behavioral explanations: you may find that you have developed strategies to avoid or escape situations in which you feel stressed. Such a pattern of behavior may not be realistic or sustainable as a solution. In fact, this can make things worse.

What keeps stress going?

Stress may build up due to factors that are out of your control. On the other hand, you might have developed a habit of taking on too much work. You may not feel confident saying no when you are asked to take on new projects. There may be things that we can do to manage situations and prevent the stress from getting worse. Take stock of what is demanded of you. Try to realistically assess your ability to cope with these things. It may be possible to rebalance your commitments. Taking practical steps like this can help to resolve at least some of the stress that you experience.

When looking more closely at what stops us overcoming stress, it becomes clear that our thoughts, feelings and behaviors all interact and combine to keep our stress going.

Challenging unpleasant thoughts

The way we think about things has an impact on our stress levels. Many of these thoughts occur outside of our control and can be negative or unhelpful. It is therefore important to remember that they are just thoughts, without any real basis, and are not necessarily facts. Even though we may believe a lot of our unhelpful thoughts when we are feeling stressed, it is good to remember that they should be questioned as they are often based on wrong assumptions. You might have unhelpful thoughts about all kinds of things, examples include:

- About the future:
    - I'm destined to fail my exams.
    - I don't see an end to this.
    - What if my partner leaves me?

- About yourself:
    - I don't feel like I have any control.
    - I can't cope with the challenge of this project.
    - I'm not good enough.

It is clear to see how this kind of thinking might bring your mood and confidence levels down. Often people can ignore the positive aspects of life or their situation. Instead, you may focus on negative elements. This style of thinking stops us feeling good about ourselves. It can lower your confidence. For example, we may give ourselves a hard time over something we are not good at (e.g., swimming) and forget all the positive skills and qualities we do have.

- Black and white thinking.
- Perfectionism.
- All or nothing.
- Should thinking.

Sometimes people only see things as black and white with no gray area or in-between. Having this polarized view can lead some people into setting themselves impossibly high standards, being overly critical and struggling to recognize any achievement due to their perfectionism.

- She must hate me.
- I should always get full marks.

You can challenge your unhelpful thoughts by asking these questions:

- Is there another way of looking at this situation?
- Is there any evidence that contradicts this thought?
- What are the pros and cons of thinking in this way?

Looking after yourself

Taking steps toward a healthy lifestyle can have a real impact on our stress levels. On the other hand, unhealthy habits can put your health at risk. It can be a real challenge to overcome some habits or behaviors. Focusing on the benefits of positive change may boost motivation.

Drugs: many drugs have a sedative or stimulant effect on the body which can have an impact on your sleep and mood. Some people use recreational drugs as a distraction, to avoid thinking about or facing problems. Using such substances can be damaging and can make things worse. Developing a habit of regular or increasing use can lead to a pattern of addictive substance misuse.

Alcohol: alcohol can impact your ability to cope and control behaviors. This can be unhelpful if you are trying to overcome problems with anger or anxiety. It can also interfere with your mood and the quality of your sleep. You might think that consuming alcohol would help you sleep. In fact, as your body processes alcohol overnight, it can wake you up. Unfortunately, this approach can be damaging and can make things worse. Drinking a lot and often can lead to a pattern of addictive substance misuse.

Caffeine: caffeine can trigger a reaction that is similar to the symptoms of anxiety. It can also reduce the quality of sleep. It is best not to have anything caffeinated within a couple of hours of bedtime. Most coffee, tea, energy drinks and some sodas contain caffeine.

Exercise: keeping fit and active can improve your physical health, mood and ability to cope with problems. Try to get some gentle exercise each week.

Healthy eating: what you eat and drink can have a significant impact on your mood, sleep and physical health. Consider making changes toward having a balanced, nutritious diet. Try to eat regular meals and stay hydrated.

Routine: having a consistent routine can help give structure to your life. Examples as follows:

- Celebrate small victories.
- Read funny books.
- Take control; there is a solution to every problem.

- Do something you enjoy each day.
- If you start to feel discouragement remind yourself that all your efforts matter, this will also motivate you.
- Make yourself laugh. Laughter is an excellent antidote to stress.
    - Watch comedies.
    - Call or message a friend or associate who makes you laugh.
- Build self-confidence: self-confidence is extremely important in almost every aspect of our lives, yet so many people struggle to find it. Sadly, this can be a vicious circle; people who lack self-confidence can find it difficult to become successful.

Stress and anxiety

Isn't it normal to feel anxious? Anxiety is something we all experience from time to time. It is a normal response to situations that we see as threatening to us. If we had to go to the dentist to get a tooth extracted, it would be natural to feel anxious. Anxiety at certain times can even be helpful in some situations such as when we need to perform well. Some anxiety is not helpful for the following reasons:

- When anxiety is severe and goes on for a long time it can stop people doing what they want to do.

- Symptoms of anxiety, while not dangerous, can be uncomfortable.
- Symptoms can also be frightening particularly if someone does not know that these symptoms are just signs of anxiety.

Anxiety can affect us in at least four different ways, as follows:

- The way we think.
- The way we feel.
- The way our body works.
- The way we behave.

You may be able to tell if you are suffering from anxiety if you regularly experience these four symptoms.

How you think

- Thoughts racing.
- Can't concentrate.
- Constant worrying.
- Mind jumping from one thing to another.

Common thoughts

- I'm going to make a fool of myself.
- I'm losing control.
- I can't cope.
- I'm going to faint.

How you feel

- Tense, stressed, on edge, unsettled.
- Panicky.

- Nervous, worried, frightened.
- Woozy, detached.

What happens to your body

- Chest feels tight or painful.
- Feeling jumpy or restless.
- Sweating.
- Breathing changes.
- Tense muscles.

What you do

- Pace up and down.
- Drink more.
- Avoid feared situations.
- Snappy and irritable behavior.
- Can't sit and relax.
- Smoke more.

What causes anxiety?

There may be many reasons why a person becomes anxious. Some of which include:

a. Some people may have an anxious personality and have learned to worry.

b. Others may be under pressure at home because of bills or debt, for example.

c. Others may have a series of stressful life events to cope with; for example, divorce and bereavement.

How can you manage your anxiety better?

Anxiety is not an illness and so can't be cured. If we can break out of the vicious circle, however, we can learn ways of reducing our anxiety and making it more manageable. We can work on at least four different areas.

1. Altering our thoughts related to anxiety: We have seen the role that thoughts have in keeping the vicious circle of anxiety going. To help alter our thoughts related to anxiety we can ask ourselves the following questions:
   - What are the thoughts that most often go through your mind?
   - Do you have any pictures of what might happen?
   - Are there any thoughts that make you feel worse?

The sorts of thoughts that make people feel anxious can come and go in a flash and may be so much of a habit that they are automatic. They may be so familiar that they just feel like part of you.

2. Understanding anxiety: Is your anxiety related to certain situations, places or people? Is it worse at particular times of the day? Are there realistic worries you have that would make anyone anxious?

Keeping an anxiety diary card can be useful to tackle your anxiety. Rate your anxiety from 0-5. Note down what seems important. What were you thinking about? Who were you with? What were you doing? And so on.

If you become aware that you have a realistic worry or problem that you feel may be causing you anxiety, a problem-solving approach may help.

A good way to begin is to write down a problem. Define it as clearly as possible. Next, write down as many possible solutions as you can. It doesn't matter how silly you may think the solutions are; the point is to think of as many as you can. Try to think how you have solved similar problems in the past.

Choose what seems like the best solution and write down all the steps it would take to achieve that solution. Why might this help? What might go wrong? Often it is helpful to think of a plan to cope with this. Your anxiety might reduce.

These days life is often stressful, and it is easy for pressures to build up. We can't always control the stress that comes from outside, but we can find ways to reduce the pressure we put on ourselves.

- Make sure you have time for things you enjoy.
- Make sure you get enough sleep.
- Try to identify situations you find stressful by noticing the beginning of tension.
- Take steps to tackle what it is about these situations that you find stressful.
- Learn to relax.

3. Reducing physical symptoms – relaxation: Once you have noticed early signs of tensions you can prevent anxiety becoming too severe by using relaxation techniques. Some people can relax through reading a book or listening to music. For others, it is more helpful to have a set of exercises to follow. Some people might find yoga classes most helpful. Relaxation is a skill like any other which needs to be learned and takes time.

   To make the best use of relaxation you need to:

   - Practice regularly.
   - Learn to relax without having to tense muscles.
   - Start to use relaxation in everyday situations.
   - Develop a more relaxed lifestyle.

Keep a note of how anxious you feel before and after relaxation, rating your anxiety from 0-5.

Over-breathing is very common. When someone becomes anxious, changes occur in their breathing. They can begin to gulp air, thinking that they are going to suffocate, or can begin to breathe really quickly. This has the effect of making them feel dizzy and therefore more anxious.

Try to recognize if you are doing this and slow your breathing down. Getting into a regular rhythm of "in two, three and out two, three" will soon return your breathing to normal. Some people find it helpful to use the mind wide open class to control their breathing. Other people have found cupped hands helpful. For this to work, you must be in a comfortable position.

If you take your mind off your symptoms, you will find that the symptoms often disappear. Try to look around you. Again you need to distance yourself for at least three minutes before symptoms will begin to reduce.

While relaxation, breathing exercises and distraction techniques can help reduce anxiety, it is vitally important to realize that anxiety is not harmful or dangerous. Even if we did not use these techniques, nothing awful would happen. Anxiety cannot harm us, but it can be uncomfortable. These techniques can help reduce this discomfort.

4. Changing behavior related to anxiety:
    - Set yourself very small and realistic goals.
    - Try to recognize when you are avoiding things and wherever possible try to tackle these fears, not all at once but in a gradual way.
    - Try to do things to test out whether your anxious thoughts are realistic.
    - People not only avoid situations and try to escape but they often also do things to make themselves feel safe; for example, lying down. This safety may help at the time, but it also helps to keep the anxiety going because the anxious person never learns that nothing

awful would have happened if they didn't lie down to relax. It really is very important to recognize that the more you avoid something, the more difficult it will seem to overcome, which will, in turn, make you more anxious.

Self-esteem

Self-esteem is our ability to value ourselves. It is slightly different from self-confidence, which refers to our sense of being able to do something successfully. Self-esteem is the overall opinion we have of ourselves. We can have a tendency to trap ourselves in the way we see and think about ourselves.

Low self-esteem can be most easily recognized by the negative statements you make about or believe about yourself. Pay attention to beliefs about yourself that you accept without question.

Our experiences, often but not exclusively, as children provide the mold for our self-esteem and set down the conclusions we make about ourselves. It is important to be open-minded and begin to view these negative self-statements as a matter of opinion, and as such, open question and debate.

To consider the roots of your self-esteem and accept the conclusion you have drawn about yourself is an understandable reaction to your unique life experience. We know experiences like excessive criticism, neglect, punishment, being different, being bullied, or hardship can contribute to low self-esteem in some people.

Have a think about memories, specific situations or experiences that might help you build a better understanding of you. The responsibility to change can be yours no matter how difficult your past has been. The means to begin to change what you want to change is certainly within your grasp.

Motivation

When you are first considering a change you might feel keen to take action, but sometimes you merely want to think about it, and at other times you just want to stay the same. These are normal experiences when you begin to think about changing.

Take your time and ask yourself:

- What is important to me?
- What is not important to me?
- What do you predict will happen if you do change?
- What is your low self-esteem affecting and in what way?
- Is there anything at risk if you do change?

Learn to challenge yourself

We know how we feel is strongly linked with how we think. Streams of thoughts are running through our minds almost constantly, and often we are completely unaware of them! When the content of these thoughts leads us to feel bad we call them "negative automatic thoughts," because they quite simply pop into our heads without any sense of being within our control. It is the unquestioning acceptance of your thoughts as your truth that helps your critical self survive and thrive. Learning to "tune in" to our critic and capture our thoughts is the basis for questioning their validity. This requires practice, but to begin with simply be aware of a change in how you feel — for example, sad, then ask yourself "what was I thinking about just then?" Typical mistakes in our thinking might be:

- Mind reading – thinking you know what someone thinks without checking it out by asking.
- Seeing everything as black or white, viewing situations or people as good or bad, not recognizing the shades of gray.
- Ignoring positive information about yourself or a situation.
- Exaggerating the negative (getting a situation out of perspective).

As you can now realize, self-esteem takes root over time, and it is likely to take you months if not years to begin to shake these roots. To begin with, remember that these thoughts are your perception. In order to loosen its grip and improve your emotional wellbeing, regard it as an opinion, not a statement of fact.

Start by thinking of some of your experiences that don't fit with your negative view of yourself. Our culture and the messages we heard as we were growing up often encouraged modesty. Developing a way of checking out the accuracy of our thoughts is a crucial element of beginning to counter your negative view of yourself, but it is unlikely to be helpful on its own. It requires the additional ingredient of behavior change. This is the challenge that requires commitment and determination to face a familiar situation differently.

Once you have recognized aspects of your behavior that protect you from exposing your worst fears, select a small part that you feel able to change. Making changes requires you to be open to taking risks and facing some disappointment. Lasting change will take root with the small steps you take along the way. Consider what might happen, then put it to the test, Check out how accurate your prediction is. What do you notice and what can you learn from this situation and others?

Some possible tools to develop self-esteem

- Figure out what your problem is.
- Figure out who you are.
- Decide what you can and can't control.
- Accept responsibility.
- Make anxiety your ally.
- Recognize that mistakes are opportunities.
- Compete to improve yourself.
- Be ambitious.

- Be brave and take risks.
- Think and speak positively.
- Learn something new.
- Spend time investing in your personal growth.
- Smile and be courteous.
- Keep good company.
- Reward yourself.
- Don't accept messages that damage your own self-esteem.
- Any thoughts that take us away from a positive feeling are not worth having or defending.
- The moment you hear a critical remark, ask yourself "what is on this person's screen?"
- Remember that all criticism shares one characteristic, it is unwelcome, but you never owe a critic your self-esteem.
- Remember a small success can bring big feelings of competence.

Compassion for yourself

Learning to develop tolerance and compassion for yourself is a vital skill for your general and emotional wellbeing. People with low self-esteem are often harshly critical of themselves, placing expectations on themselves that do not match their expectations of others.

Many people's lives are busy with obligations to others – children, employers, partners and parents. The continual pattern of attending to others and ignoring yourself is likely to keep low self-esteem going, create stress, frustration and low mood.

Remember your self-esteem did not develop overnight, and neither will it improve overnight. There is no such miracle treatment. Remember only you have the control to be the person you are capable of being. Learn to accept yourself with no strings attached.

Part Four

The Love-Response Helper

The power of grounding techniques and emotional intelligence

Grounding is a technique that helps keep a person to the here and now. It helps reorientate a person in the present and reality. It can help you to regain your mental focus from an intensely emotional state.

Although grounding does not solve the problem that is contributing to your unpleasant emotions, it does provide a temporary way to gain control over your feelings and prevent things from getting worse. Grounding anchors you, gives you a chance to calm down and allows you to eventually return and address the problem that is triggering the unpleasant emotions to begin with. And grounding can be done any time, anywhere and no one has to know.

Ways of grounding

There are three types of grounding:

1. Mental (focusing your mind).
2. Physical (focusing your senses).
3. Soothing (talking to yourself in a very kind way).

Many people who have been abused struggle with either feeling too much (overwhelming emotions and memories), or too little (numbing disassociation). In grounding, you attain balance between the two – conscious of reality and the ability to tolerate it.

There are a few things that can help grounding be successful in therapy. Grounding techniques can seem very simple to do but are not always easy to do in the moment, so practicing often can be helpful. Making grounding a regular part of your therapy sessions with clients with Post Traumatic Stress Disorder (PTSD) will make it easier for them to engage, as well as giving those clients many chances to experience how it helps. Giving clients handouts so that they can easily remember what to do on their own really helps, don't you think?

In the past, trauma survivors were encouraged to speak about their abuse in the belief that this catharsis would be healing. Sometimes this instead leads to traumatization rather than mastery of the material or healing.

A skilled therapist can help the client to learn grounding skills so that they can be present enough to develop a whole range of self-care strategies, which is crucial.

Processing done from a very disassociated state is not useful in trauma work. Neither is the goal to be so overwhelmed by the feelings that you feel retraumatized. Once you are present, you also need to learn other means of managing the feelings and thoughts associated with traumatic memories.

Everyone is different. Different grounding techniques will work for different people. The following are some general categories and ideas. Exploring the pros and cons of various approaches with your therapist can be useful.

Grounding often takes the form of focusing on the present by tuning into it via all of your senses; for example, one technique could involve focusing on a sound you hear right now, or a physical sensation (what is the texture of the chair you are sitting on?).

Diaphragmatic or deep breathing: trauma survivors often hold their breath or breathe very shallowly. This, in turn, deprives you of oxygen which can make anxiety more intense. Stopping and focusing on deepening and slowing your breathing can bring you back to the moment.

Grounding and emotion management skills can help you proceed with the work of trauma therapy in a manner that feels empowering instead of re-traumatizing. Although the ultimate benefits of practicing grounding techniques will come from experience itself, the future for practicing and becoming competent in using grounding techniques looks promising.

Emotional intelligence for productivity, creativity, resilience, and happiness

Emotional intelligence definitions

"A type of social intelligence that involves the ability to monitor one's own emotions, to discriminate among them and to use the information to guide one's thinking and actions." *(Salovey and Mayer, 1990)*

"The capacity for recognizing our own feelings and those for motivating ourselves, and for managing emotions well in ourselves and in our relationships." *(Goleman, 1999)*

Why does emotional intelligence matter?

- For a start, for performers in all jobs, in every field, emotional competence is twice as important as purely cognitive abilities.
- For success at the highest levels, in leadership positions, emotional competence accounts for virtually the entire advantage. (*Goleman – Hey/McBer research)*

Misconceptions about emotional intelligence

1. Emotional intelligence does not merely mean "being nice."
2. Emotional intelligence does not mean giving free rein to feelings.
3. Women are smarter than men when it comes to emotional intelligence.

Emotional intelligence and emotional competencies

The five dimensions of emotional intelligence:

1. Self-awareness.
2. Self-regulation.
3. Self-motivation.
4. Empathy.
5. Social skills.

Self-awareness

- Emotional awareness (mindfulness).
- Accurate self-assessment.
- Self-confidence.

Self-regulation

- Self-control.
- Trustworthiness.
- Conscientiousness.
- Adaptability.
- Innovation.

Social skills

- Influence.
- Communication.
- Leadership.
- Change catalyst.
- Conflict management.
- Building bonds.
- Collaboration and cooperation.
- Team capabilities.

"The ingredients for outstanding performance require only that we have strengths in a given number of these competencies, typically at least six or so, and that the strengths be spread across all five areas of emotional intelligence." *(Goleman, 1998)*

Principles of emotional intelligence

- Emotion is information – mainly about people and not about moods.
- We can try to ignore emotion, but it doesn't work.
- We can try to hide emotion, but we aren't as good as we think.
- Decisions must incorporate emotion to be effective.
- Emotions follow logical patterns.

Changing negative state

- Future pace.
- Visualization.
- Remember a joke.
- Change your body language.
- Take a brisk walk.
- Write it down.

Ask the right questions

- What can you do with the emotions? Do they need to be modified?
- How can you manage these feelings so they are used adaptively in decision making and in motivating behavior?

- How do you feel? How strongly?
- What are you thinking about?
- How are these feelings influencing your thoughts?
- Why do you feel this way?
- What was the cause?
- How have these feelings progressed?
- Is it natural to fear?
- Where does fear come from?
- Why flight or fight?
- Why do we have emotions?
- Wouldn't it be much better just to let our emotions go away?

Emotions

Emotions can define our lives and are signals to take action.

Emotional needs

Without any doubt we need our emotions – and we have emotional needs. These include:

- Connections to others emotionally.
- Security.
- Attention – to give and receive.
- Belonging – in a group or society.
- Intimacy – friendship.
- Uncertainty.
- Status.

Types of emotions

- **Primeval (reactive):**
  - Fight and flight.
  - Defensive rage.
  - Survival instincts.
  - Mother and baby.
  - Baby and mother.
  - Love and jealousy.
  - Shame and guilt.
- **Routine emotions include:**
  - Anger.
  - Sadness.
  - Happiness.
  - Worry.
  - Calmness.
  - Love.
  - Agitation.
  - Fear.
  - Confidence.
  - Guilt.
  - Confusion.
- **Reflective emotions:**
  - Includes many of the routine emotions, and like the primeval emotions, they are stimulated by our conscious thoughts, may be retained subconsciously and later restimulated as a traumatic response.

How we respond to emotions and the role of the amygdala

- Senses detect something happening which could affect our wellbeing or safety.
- Switch in our brain affects physical responses.
- Emotional center (amygdala), in the limbic system.
    - Center for emotional nervous system – primeval response system (flight or fight response).
- Neocortex.
    - (New brain) the higher comprehension and analytical center of the brain – command center for the amygdala which sends instructions for physical actions.

The three pillars of emotional trauma therapy (Ruden R.)

1. Psychotherapies.
2. Psychopharmacologies.
3. Psychosensory therapies.

Psychotherapies

These are some popular forms of psychotherapy, counseling therapy:

- Cognitive behavioral.
- Rational-emotive therapy.
- Person-centered therapy.

- Psychodynamic.
- Psychoanalytical.
- Gestalt.
- Solution focus.
- Dialectical behavior.
- Mindfulness-based cognitive therapy.

Psychopharmacologies

Listed below are some psychopharmacological drug classes:

- Mood stabilizers.
- Pain relievers.
- Antidepressants.
- Anti-anxiety.
- Anti-compulsive.
- Anti-hallucinatory.

Psychosensory therapies

Dr. Ruden lists psychosensory therapies as follows:

- Havening.
- Meridian techniques (EFT/TFT).
- Eye movement desensitization and reprocessing (EMDR).

Remember

"Everyone falls in love sometimes."

"True love never dies, no matter how hard you try."

"Let us not love in word or talk but in deed and in truth."

"Let love and faithfulness never leave you, bind them around your neck, write them on the tablet of your heart." (Proverbs 3:3)

"Real love doesn't care about your body type, model looks or wallet size. It only cares about what is inside."

"A loving heart is the truest wisdom."

"Love is a fruit in season at all times and within reach of every hand." (Mother Teresa)

"Love is a fabric which never fades, no matter how often it is washed in the water of adversity and grief."

"Love is of all passions the strongest, for it attacks simultaneously the head, the heart and the senses."

"Love is to love someone for who they are, who they were, and who they will be."

"You can have true happiness in life. To love and to be loved."

"Where there is love there is life."

"Love is the only sane satisfactory answer to the problem of human existence."

"We all live with the objective of being happy; our lives are all different and yet the same." (Anne Frank)

"Be happy with what you have. Be excited about what you want."

"Nobody really cares if you're miserable, so you might as well be happy."

"One of the simplest ways to stay healthy is by letting go of the things that make you sad."

"Without love, we are nothing but organic molecules circling around the sun."

"Love is the secret you unmask yourself to find; it is the foundation of the spiritual life, the destination where all roads of the journey lead."

"Happiness always looks small while you can hold it in your hands, but let it go, and you learn at once how big and precious it is."

"The loving mind recognizes the value and beauty in every living thing."

"A friend is one that knows you as you are, understands where you have been, accepts what you have become, and still gently allows you to grow." (William Shakespeare).

"You can't change how people feel about you, so don't try. Just live your life and be happy."

"Life only comes around once, so do whatever makes you happy and be whoever makes you smile."

"There are so many beautiful reasons to be happy."

"Start each day with a grateful heart."

"Always believe that something wonderful is about to happen."

"One of the simplest ways to be happy is letting go of the things that make you sad."

"Always strive to be happy because you never know who is falling in love with your smile."

"Be happy without comparing yourself to others."

"Be the reason someone smiles today."

"Keep smiling and one day life will get tired of upsetting you."

"Happiness is always knocking on your door, you just have to let it in."

"A smile is the most beautiful thing you can wear."

"Every day holds the possibility of a wonderful miracle."

"A good friendship starts with good communication."

"Do good for others, and it will come back in unexpected ways."

"Challenges make us more responsible. Always remember life without challenges is a life without success."

"We always work for a better tomorrow. But when tomorrow comes, instead of enjoying, we again think of a better tomorrow! Let's have a better day."

"Stay positive, things you are waiting for tend to arrive at the most unexpected moments."

"Be happy with nothing, and you will be happy with everything."

"One kind word can change someone's day."

"Everyone you meet is fighting a battle you know nothing about. Always be kind."

"How beautiful a day can be when love touches it."

"Be careful with your words. Once they are said, they can only be forgiven, not forgotten."

"Kindness is a gift everyone can afford to give."

"Kind words can be short and easy to speak, but their echoes are truly endless." (Mother Teresa)

"Help people even when you know they cannot help you back."

"Our days are happier when we give others a bit of our heart rather than a piece of our mind."

"It is only compassion, acceptance, kindness and love that can change the human heart."

"Be someone's sunshine when their skies are gray."

"Our heart is the garden that always has room for the flowers of kindness and friendships to bloom."

"Carry out a random act of kindness, with no expectations of reward, safe in the knowledge that one day someone might do the same for you." (Princess Diana)

"What wisdom can you find that is greater than kindness?" (Jean Jacques)

"Use your voice for kindness, your ears for compassion, your hands for charity, your mind for truth, and your heart for love."

"Kindness makes you the most beautiful person in the world no matter what you look like."

"Love should be everything or not at all."

"Let's give love a try and make hatred be our enemies."

Glossary of terms

Abuse:	A person subjecting or exposing another person to behavior that may result in trauma.
Acceptance:	Occurs when a situation or scenario is acknowledged and accepted by an individual. It is typically used in reference to the acknowledgment and assent to a negative situation.
Ambitious:	Having or showing a strong desire and determination to succeed.
Anger:	Is an emotion characterized by antagonism toward someone or something you feel has deliberately done you wrong.
Assertiveness:	Is the quality of being self-assured and confident without being aggressive.
Attitudes:	A predisposition or a tendency to respond positively or negatively toward a certain object, idea, person or situation.
Behavior:	How one acts or conducts oneself toward others.
Belonging:	Means acceptance as a member or part. A sense of belonging is a human need, just like the need for water, food and good air.
Care:	The provision of what is necessary for the health, welfare, maintenance and protection of someone or something.

Client-centered: Is a counseling approach that requires the client to take an active role in his or her treatment with the therapist being non-directive and supportive.

Clinical: A branch of psychology concerned with the assessment and treatment of mental illness and behavioral problems.

Cognition: The study of mental processes such as attention, language use, memory, perceptions, problem solving and thinking.

Confidence: Having the belief to succeed.

Depressed: A common and serious medical condition that negatively affects how we think and act.

Disorder: A psychological dysfunction in an individual.

Effective: Successful in producing a desired or intended result.

Embrace: To hold or clasp someone in your arms as a way of expecting love or friendship.

Emotions: Is a feeling such as happiness, love, fear, anger or hatred which can be caused by the situation that you are in or the people you are with.

Empathy: Is the experience of understanding another person's condition from their perspective. You place yourself in their shoes and feel what they are feeling.

Emptiness:	Is a lack of connectedness to the world and to others.
Encouragement:	The action of giving someone support, confidence or hope.
Fear:	An unpleasant and often strong emotion caused by awareness of unemployment, divorce, danger, etc.
Feelings:	An emotional state or reaction, examples include affections, fondness, warmth, fancy.
Forgive:	A deliberate decision to release feelings of resentment or revenge toward a person who has harmed you.
Gestalt:	The perception and behavior from the standpoint of an individual's response to configurational whole with stress on the uniformity of psychological and physiological events and rejection of analysis into discrete events or stimulus and response.
Goals:	The result or achievement toward which effort is directed.
Happiness:	Positive or pleasant emotions ranging from contentment to intense joy. It is also a mental state of wellbeing.
Hatred:	Is an extremely strong feeling of dislike for someone or something.
Health:	The state of being free from illness or injury.

Helpful: Giving positive assistance or serving a useful function; for example, being kind, friendly or supportive.

Hope: A feeling of expectation and desire for a particular thing to happen.

Kindness: The quality of being generous and considerate.

Loneliness: Is the state of being alone and feeling sad about it.

Love: A feeling of warm personal attachment or deep affection.

Loyalty: A person who is loyal remains firm in their friendship or support for a person or thing.

Meditation: Turning your attention away from distracting thoughts and focusing on the present moment.

Mindfulness: Bringing one's complete attention to the present experience on a moment-to-moment basis.

Motivation: The process that initiates, guides and maintains goal-orientated behavior. Motivation is what causes us to action how we behave.

Neurosis: A psychological state characterized by excessive anxiety or insecurity without evidence of neurological disease, sometimes accompanied by defensive or immature behaviors.

Patience: The ability to tolerate or accept delay problems without becoming annoyed or anxious.

Pleasant:	Someone or something that is agreeable, enjoyable or likable.
Potential:	To show the capacity to develop into sometime in the future.
Psyche:	The totality of the human mind, conscious and unconscious.
Quality:	The degree of excellence of something.
Relationships:	The way in which two or more people or things are connected, or the state of being connected.
Relaxed:	Free from tension and anxiety.
Resilience:	The ability to recover from or adjust easily to misfortune or change.
Respect:	A feeling of deep admiration for someone or something elicited by their abilities.
Reward:	A thing given in recognition of service, effort or an achievement. It is also something that is given in return for good or evil done or received.
Self-care:	Is any necessary human regulatory function which is under individual control. It is essential to safeguarding your wellbeing.
Self-esteem:	Is used to describe a person's overall sense of self-worth or personal value. It can involve a variety of beliefs about the self, such as the appraisal of one's own appearance, beliefs, emotions, and behavior.

Self-hatred:	The feelings of one who hates, extreme dislike, extreme aversion or hostility.
Self-image:	The idea, conception or mental image one has of oneself.
Shame:	The painful feeling arising from the consciousness of something dishonorable, improper, regretful.
Stress:	The body's way of responding to any kind of demand.
Therapy:	Treatment intended to relieve or heal a disorder.
Thoughts:	An idea or opinion produced by thinking or occurring suddenly in the mind.
Unique:	Having no like or equal, incomparable.
Value:	A belief or principle that a person or group has that determines what is correct, desirable and proper.

References

Cooke, N., Formal, Informal, Mindfulness Practice.

Evans, M. T., Blog/healing resources.

Hays and Davis (2011), Mindfulness definition.

Johnson, S., Perseus Publishing (2014), *The Love Secret* p. 12-13.

Kilical, B., Social love workshop/article.

Larcombe, M., How to become unconditionally loving article.

Linehan, M. M., Guildford Press (2015), *DBT Skills Training Manual: What is Mindfulness* p. 151.

McKenna, P., Bantam Press, (2011), *I Can Make You Happy,* p. 105, p. 112, p. 182.

Rankin, L., Hay House Publishing (2015), *The Fear Cure,* p.p. 179-180, p. 190, p. 192, p. 194.

Selhub, E. M., What is Love-Response article.

Truman, D., The Living Love Fellowship article.

Young, K., Treating Trauma article.

About the author

Wayne Lindsey is a therapeutic counselor and a mindfulness trainer. He enjoys go-karting, salsa dancing and singing at weddings and other party functions.